McDonnell Douglas
F-4
Phantom II

McDonnell Douglas
F-4
Phantom II
ROBERT F. DORR

OSPREY AIR COMBAT

Published in 1984 by Osprey Publishing Limited
12–14 Long Acre, London WC2E 9LP
Member company of the George Philip Group
© Robert F Dorr 1984

Sole distributors for the USA

Osceola, Wisconsin 54020, USA

British Library Cataloguing in Publication Data

Dorr, Robert F.
   F-4 Phantom II.—(Osprey air combat series)
   1. Phantom (Fighter planes)
   I. Title
   623.74'64   UG1242.F5
ISBN 0-85045-587-1

Editor Dennis Baldry

Printed in Spain

Contents

For Curtis

Introduction

Colonel Charles E Yeager shook my hand, grinned, and said he'd heard that I liked the F-4 Phantom. We huddled in a corridor in the American Embassy in Seoul, warrior and diplomat. A lot of shooting was going on and Yeager's profession seemed to have eclipsed mine.

It was January 1968. The North Koreans had begun commando raids on the south and had captured our intelligence ship *Pueblo*. We hadn't had a single tactical jet fighter ready for action.

From Seymour Johnson AFB in the pine forests of North Carolina, F-4D Phantom squadrons of Yeager's 4th Tactical Fighter Wing deployed to Korea so rapidly that crews arrived at Kunsan Air Base with their flight suits, their shaving gear, their socks. Kunsan was a place of frozen mud, howling wind and biting ice storms, the winter so harsh that even the bar girls from town stayed away; the men threw up tents and the Phantoms flew in a blizzard. It took the right stuff, the stuff of men who take their aircraft to war in farflung places as a matter of tradition. At Kunsan, for months, American Phantoms stared down North Korea's MiG-21s, none dared engage, and the *Pueblo* crew came home for Christmas. Again, the warrior had had to wrest success where the diplomat could not. Again, as happened so often, the despatch of a wing of F-4 Phantoms had become the final resort on the cutting edge of American policy.

'Yeah, I like the F-4 too,' said Yeager. 'Good plane.' He does not say much.

The other war contined, the endless war. In the late 1960s, we sensed—we *felt* rather than *knew*— that we were going to have to return to Route Package Six to settle things with Colonel Tomb. In the parched heat at Davis-Monthan AFB near Tucson, an American fighter wing commander walked in small circles, pondering his experience in three wars, pondering Tomb's, counselling a young wife. She had sought him out. Her man, her Phantom front-seater, was training over the Arizona desert to do battle in the skies of North Vietnam. There was a bombing halt. There were negotiations. She *had* to know. Would her young captain find himself pitted against the heaviest defences the world has ever known, against the enemy's wily and aggressive fighter wing commander, against men in MiGs bent on killing him? Or would the bombing halt hold? Col Andrew Baird, who does not say much either, did not believe, just as Col Yeager could not have believed, that my colleagues were going to settle it. Baird said to Mary Ackerman:

'*Maybe I'm wrong. Maybe our diplomats in Paris will wrap it up before I have to take these men back to Hanoi. But my sense of history tells me that some of these men will bleed and die before we put this one away. It has always been so . . .*'

Not everything about Baird's airplane was perfect. Early F-4Cs sprang wing tank leaks that required resealing after each flight. Eighty-five of them developed cracked ribs on outer wing panels. The F-4C and RF-4C were at times grounded due to dripping potting compound. Early F-4Es had a high rate of engine stalls and flameouts. Teething problems with missile armament continued well past the first decade of the Phantom's service life. Such are the vicissitudes typical of any major aircraft type. They do not detract from the simple truth that the Phantom was, and is, the finest fighter of its era.

When men in Phantoms returned to North Vietnam, they prevailed. They won in battle the settlement the policymakers wanted. Today, Phantoms prowl the NATO frontier and the Korean DMZ. Phantoms fly in the Falklands. So long as free men remain willing to use force of

Pistol-packing (.38 Smith & Wesson) Col Robin Olds uses stencil and spray paint to apply his second MiG kill to 8th Tactical Fighter Wing 'Wolfpack' F-4C Phantom (63-7668) on 4 May 1967
(US Air Force)

TITLE PAGES
F-4J Phantom (155552) of the 'Diamondbacks' of VF-102 from the USS Independence *(CVA-62) during Atlantic Fleet operations in September 1970. The F-4J flying lead is at top right of picture*
(US Navy)

arms where need is, the Phantom has an assured role for years to come.

It is becoming habitual, if premature, to speak of the Phantom in the past tense. To be sure, a major segment of the Phantom story *is* history now. Few have summed it up more aptly than Capt Gerald G O'Rourke, who was present at the creation:

'I doubt that we ever had a single aircraft design that so significantly marked a transition, that was (and still is) so widely used in so many front-line roles, and that had so many anomalies in its developmental history. It wasn't even supposed to be a fighter. It wasn't supposed to be a land-based aircraft. It wasn't intended to foster a whole new breed of aviation first-liners (RIOs, GIBs, WSOs). Yet it did all of these things and so many more.

'As I think back on it, the real key (if there was one) was not necessarily the fine airframe. The engines have to get a lot of credit, though they didn't come from our best-known engine manufacturer. The radar was, I think, the major factor in establishing historical claims for the airplane. Looking back, it was a fascinating era of tumultous progress in some areas and moribund traditionalism in others.

'Good times, however. Real challenges, mind-boggling achievements and tragic failures, all mixed in together and often difficult to separate among the many people involved . . .'

This is a book about an American warplane, by an American author, for a British publisher, in an international world. It is for Phantom crews and for air enthusiasts, so each is asked to accept the compromises in style needed for the other. Phantom crews care little about block numbers, serials, callsigns. They often fail to record these for history. They will read them here, nonetheless. The enthusiast may have difficulty with the jargon of those who fly and fight and must accept that, in this book at least, you pickle off the tanks rather than jettisoning them. A glossary is appended. Military ranks are given for the time covered.

No book can reveal all about five thousand airframes, in fifteen countries, waging several wars over twenty-seven years. Not every squadron is mentioned here and not every crewman, not when more than nine thousand men have logged 1,000 hours in the Phantom. Though air battles over North Vietnam are recounted, the 1965–73 air-to-ground war fought inside South Vietnam by airmen and Marines in Phantoms is touched upon only briefly. Readers interested in the Phantom in British service will find a comprehensive account in a companion volume, *McDonnell Douglas F-4K and F-4M Phantom*, by Michael Burns.

This volume contains about 12,000 items of fact. Errors are the sole responsibility of the author. The effort would have been impossible, however, without the generous help of many who assisted.

I have a lifetime debt to Jerome B Curtis, for whom this is the last cut and to whom this work is dedicated. I am indebted to Michael A France, my mentor on matters F-4, who knows more about Phantoms than anybody, and to Robert S (Beaver) Blake, that unique fixture of the McDonnell Aircraft Company, who knows more about Phantoms than Mike. Portions of chapters one and seven appeared in *Aviation News* and *Scale Aircraft Modelling*, and I am grateful to Alan W Hall for allowing me to expand on them here. Thanks are due to Reed Duncan, who did the section on Israel.

Assistance in the preparation of this work was provided by the Department of State, Headquarters United States Air Force, Headquarters Third Air Force, and numerous American military units. Assistance also came from the McDonnell Douglas Corporation and many other firms in the aerospace field.

I especially want to thank Robert J Archer, Paul Auerswald, Col Andrew Baird, the editor Dennis Baldry, Robert L Burns, Michael A Burton, Hugh Campbell, Commodore Norman D Campbell, Col Kenneth W Cordier, Lt Col John D Cummings, 'Deep Throat,' Robert P Dorr, Col Robert F Foxworth, James W Freidhoff, Sqn Ldr Ian B Hamilton, Col G F Robert Hanke, Donald L Jay, Capt Johnny R Jones, Martin Judge, M J Kasiuba, Don Linn, Robert C Little, David W Menard, Lt Gen Thomas H Miller, George S Mills, Col Jack D Morris, Capt David Moss, Capt Gerald G O'Rourke, Lt Col Donald S Pickard, Eric Renth, Frederick W Roos, Capt James Rotramel, Cdr Michael A Ruth, Don Spering, Karen Stubberfield, James T Sullivan, Norman Taylor, Walter Trimborn, Col Alfred H Uhalt, Jr, and Capt Guy Walsh.

The views expressed in this book are mine and do not necessarily reflect those of the Department of State or of the United States Air Force.

Robert F Dorr
London, March 1984

Chapter 1
Pioneering with a Prototype
The Brief, Brave Life of 142259

It was a foregone conclusion. This story would *have* to begin with a quote. At the McDonnell plant in St Louis in early May 1958, when F4H-1 Phantom II prototype 142259 was rolled out, some observer *must* have done a double-take and wondered if the thing would fly. It was a bent-wing apparition, seemingly defying every principle of aerodynamics. So the author would find an eyewitness who, at first sight, had exclaimed the only possible reaction: '*My God, somebody stepped on the blueprints!*'

That's not what happened.

'We knew we had a winner from the start,' says George S Mills, McDonnell test pilot, the second man to pilot a Phantom.

It was one of those junctures in history when innovation arrived full-blown and everybody realized it. Fighter planes were supposed to be single-seaters with guns. Everybody knew that. But in 1958, the two-seat, missile-armed Phantom was an idea whose time had come.

The first of many Phantoms, 142259 deserves a niche in history not for its own achievements—it wasn't around long enough—but simply because it *was* the first. Superlative comment on the F-4 Phantom series which followed has become commonplace. 'For a generation, Phantoms have risen from land and sea to take command of the air,' read a company advertisement. If the prototype was to survive too briefly to demonstrate its full potential, other Phantoms will remain in operational service long enough to be flown by men born the year it was rolled out.

The Beginning

The Phantom owed its creation to a decision by the McDonnell firm to seek a major role as a manufacturer of jet fighters. The company had developed the Navy's first carrier-based jet fighter, the FD-1 (later FH-1) Phantom, followed by the F2H Banshee which went to war in Korea, the lacklustre F3H Demon, and the XF-88 and F-101 series for the Air Force. As often happens, a setback led to renewed efforts: The loss in 1953 of a fighter contract which went to the Vought F8U Crusader, far from discouraging James S McDonnell's hard-working people, including key designer Herman Barkey, inspired further work toward what would become the Phantom II.

The new design began in mid-1953 as a single-place, long-range attack craft financed by the company and completed in mock-up form under the tentative designation F3H-G. 'It's never been acknowledged,' says a company employee, 'but the Phantom owes a real debt to the design work that went into the F3H Demon.' 521 Demons had been built by McDonnell from the inception of the program in 1949 to its completion in 1959.

A marriage between a shortened Demon and a swept-wing Banshee, the F3H-G had straight tailplanes and incorporated the 'Coke bottle' fuselage shape then coming into vogue for supersonic aircraft.

This proposal pioneered many of the planning phases of the 'weapon system' concept then gaining popularity. Originally intended as a single-

place, long-range attack aircraft, it was to be equipped with APQ-50 radar, armed with four 20-mm cannons, and given external store stations for various ground attack weapons.

The originally proposed powerplants were two Wright J65 engines, although even then the more powerful General Electric J79 was foreseen as a future production change to provide a programmed increase in performance.

The F3H-G design was studied by the Navy's Bureau of Aeronautics and by the Deputy Chief of Naval Operations (CNO) for Air. They requested that a formal development proposal be submitted, and this was accomplished in August 1954. This resulted in a letter of intent in October 1954 for the fabrication of two prototype and one static test aircraft. At this time, the designation of the new machine was changed to AH-1 to reflect its intended ground attack mission.

Development work moved in fits and starts. In September 1954, the Navy informed McDonnell that its proposal was too vague and asked the company to re-submit. On 14 May 1955, the CNO requested a review of the AH-1 program and was considering ceasing further development. While this hurdle was overcome by late March, the program later experienced other minor delays, some caused by difficulty in preparing engineering drawings as minor changes were constantly introduced to the new design.

During this period there were two schools of thought as to whether Navy aircraft of this type should be single-place or two-place. So McDonnell prepared both single- and two-place configurations, identical except that the two-seat version had a 150 gallon fuel cell removed from the forward fuselage to provide space for the second crewman. This fuel was replaced by expanding the external centerline tank by approximately the same volume.

Specifications were agreed to by the Navy and the manufacturer on 25 July 1955. At about the same time, the Navy authorized Chance Vought to build two prototypes of the single-seat, single-engine, missile-carrying F8U-3 fighter to compete with the McDonnell design. The McDonnell bird, now intended for all-weather fleet defence but with much of its attack capability remaining, was now specified to have:

—twin J79 engines;
—Sparrow III missile armament (a proposal for a folding-fin variant of the Sidewinder was short-lived, and provisions for four 20-mm cannons were deleted);

The real progenitor of the Phantom was McDonnell's F3H Demon, 521 of which were delivered to the Fleet in the 1950s. F3H-2N Demon 133594 is typical of these single-seat, single-engine fighters which preceded the two-man, twin-engine Phantom
(MDC)

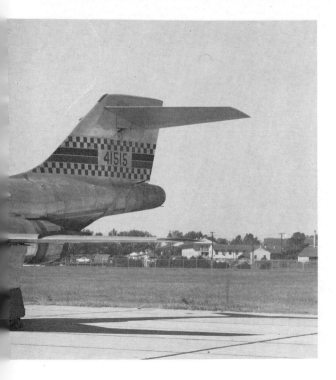

ABOVE
*A mock-up of the F4H-1 showing the two-man cockpit.
Factory-fresh Demons are lined-up in the background
(MDC)*

OPPOSITE
*Though best known for its naval fighters, McDonnell
gained valuable experience with the F-101 Voodoo for the
Phantom program. This RF-101A at Shaw AFB, South
Carolina reflects the colourful markings of 1955, but
camouflaged Voodoos would later precede the RF-4C
Phantom on photo-taking missions into North Vietnam
(Robert F Dorr)*

TOP LEFT
*The F3H-G/H mock-up at St Louis
(MDC)*

OVERLEAF
*On 28 February 1958, just before being moved to a new
location for final assembly, 142259 is being put together
with a line of F3H Demon fighters in the background.
Although it is not generally acknowledged, the Phantom
actually owes some debt to the Demon design. At this point,
the Number One Phantom is just three months away from
its first flight and it's unlikely that factory workers realize
more than 5,000 airplanes will follow
(MDC)*

—improved air intercept radar;
—a single, lightweight, semi-automatic navigation device;
—visual ground attack capability;
—maximum speed of at least Mach 2.0 with missile armament;
—a two-man crew;
—semi-submerged missile installation.

Wind tunnel tests completed in August 1956 yielded promising results. At this point, the first flight of the new aircraft was scheduled for February 1958 and then, through a company plan for overtime, was pushed ahead to December 1957. By the end of 1956, however, because of plans to shift the first flight from St Louis to Edwards Air Force Base, a March 1958 maiden flight was foreseen. These plans were changed once more in September 1957 when the Bureau of Aeronautics directed McDonnell to accomplish the first flight at St Louis in April 1958.

By the time the prototype aircraft was actually ready to fly at Lambert Field in St Louis on 27 May, more than 6.8 *million* man-hours had gone into its design and construction, and 1,500 subcontractors and suppliers from 28 states were involved in the project.

The Rollout

Painted in the standard gray-white Navy paint scheme of the time, prototype 142259 was rolled out and given a 'ramp status' examination on 8 May 1958. G79-GE-3 engines had briefly been installed in this first Phantom II, but by now it had been equipped with two YJ79-GE-3 powerplants which developed 15,600 lb (7,074 kg) static thrust at sea level. Essentially a single-seater with a non-functioning rear seat position, the first Phantom had a flush canopy, five- to eight-inch (129 to 203 mm) variable air intake inlets, and an APQ-50 radar with a 24-inch (60 cm) dish. (Beginning with the 19th production airplane, the Phantom II would employ J79-GE-8 engines, a raised canopy with better vision for the rear-seat Radar Intercept Officer, ten- to fourteen-inch variable intake inlets, and APQ-72 radar with a 32-inch (81 cm) dish).

The prototype machine was given its first taxi test on May 16, followed by another on May 23 and three separate taxi tests on May 25. Apart from a few routine 'glitches,' the first Phantom was found to be performing normally and was pronounced ready to take to the air.

The First Flights

Robert C Little, chief test pilot for McDonnell, had high hopes for the first flight. Four years earlier, the prototype F-101 Voodoo had gone supersonic on its maiden trip and Little hoped to

On 14 April 1958, McDonnell plant workers gingerly move the first Phantom, 142259, from its original location near the F3H Demon production line to another spot where final assembly and painting will be completed. The aircraft was given 'ramp status' on May 8th, completed three taxi tests on May 25th, and made its first trouble-plagued flight with Bob Little at the controls on May 27th (MDC)

OPPOSITE
Taken around the time of its roll-out from the factory on 8 May 1958, this is perhaps the best known photo of F4H-1 Phantom 142259, the first machine built (MDC)

repeat the achievement with the F4H-1.

It was not to be.

With a small group of onwatchers—among them, a General Electric employee crouched in weeds beside the runway, who snapped the first picture ever taken of a Phantom in flight—Little began his take-off roll with afterburners at a gross weight of 36,000 lb (16,363 kg). While the GE man clicked his shutter, Little noted good take-off characteristics and reduced his throttles to the military power setting. The right-hand engine developed a minor RPM oscillation which Little resolved after two or three minutes by reducing power slightly. But as his climb-out continued, the

TOP LEFT
The first of 5,201, the prototype F4H-1 Phantom (142259) at Edwards AFB, California on 17 May 1958 (William L Swisher)

During taxi trials at St Louis immediately prior to its first flight in May 1958, the initial F4H-1 Phantom (142259) sports a 'candy stripe' nose and pitot tube (MDC)

OVERLEAF
The first F4H-1 Phantom, 142259, in May 1958 (MDC)

pilot noted a more serious problem: A hydraulic warning light came on and pressure dropped abruptly to zero. *The landing gear was not fully retracted!*

Behind Bob Little, the pilot of the chase F-101, William S Ross, observed an apparent seepage of hydraulic fluid under the right wing. Little retracted the leading and trailing edge flaps with no perceptible trim change. But he was operating on one rather than two power control systems and all was not well: At 10,000 ft (3,050 m), he discontinued the climb and reduced to 370 knots IAS (685 km/h). At this time, the chase pilot reported that his nose gear door was not fully closed. Little decided, however, not to attempt to cycle the gear at this point.

Little could not enjoy the pre-arch St Louis panorama which passed beneath him shrouded by a slight haze. He was intent on the technical problem. Although getting good handling characteristics considering his power handicap, he knew now that this first flight would end less than satisfactorily. A company report, in curiously passive English, recounts the minutes that followed:

'The airplane handling qualities were briefly evaluated to 370 knots (685 km/h) IAS with satisfactory results on the lateral and longitudinal control system. Dihedral effect was mild and lateral-directional damping as a result of rudder input was good. Speed brakes were extended at 350 knots (648 km/h) IAS with no noticeable trim change. Air speed was reduced to approximately 240 knots (444 km/h) IAS where the landing gear was extended satisfactorily with no trim change. Air speed was reduced further to 200 knots (370 km/h) IAS and the leading and trailing edge flaps were extended; trim change was not perceptible to the pilot. The flight was discontinued at this time since continued operation on one power control system was inadvisable.

'Landing approach was made at 160 knots (296 km/h) IAS at approximately 81% RPM on the engines with touch-down occurring at approximately 155 knots (287 km/h) IAS. Parabrake was deployed satisfactorily and the landing roll was easily controlled with moderate wheel braking.'

The chase pilot's photos of the beautifully-painted 142259 with the Mississippi in the background depict Bob Little's historic flight and clearly show the plane with landing gear both down and up (albeit with nose gear door dangling). The pictures also indicate the day-glo red band added to the standard Navy markings, arrow-like, along the length of the upper fuselage

as well as the designation 'F4H-1' emblazoned in 26-inch (66 cm) letters on the nose.

Signed by company official E R Shields, the report on the 16-minute first flight ended on a far from cheerful note:

'Post-flight inspection revealed that a loss of hydraulic pressure was due to a hydraulic line failure at the No 2 power control system reservoir pressurization line. Inspection of the right-hand engine revealed no obvious cause of the RPM surge condition that occurred on takeoff. However, further inspection of the engine revealed foreign object damage due to the compressor blades. The engine has been rejected and is being replaced prior to the second flight which is expected on 28 May.'

If *this* was to be a 'winner' of a fighter plane, there remained hard moments ahead!

Prior to Little's second trip aloft in 142259, the right engine was replaced and the inlet ramps were re-positioned at 4 degrees. It didn't help. On the second flight—29 May 1958—the nose landing gear door remained partly open. Again, 'no high Mach number tests were possible.' Little might well have wondered if his bent-wing bird was ever to get past the speed of sound!

It did. On May 31st and June 2nd, the third and fourth flights, the Phantom reached Mach numbers from 1.30 to 1.68. Reported company official J F Goodrich: 'The airplane has been put on work status to correct cockpit leakage in order

LEFT
In about May 1958, Robert C Little climbs aboard the very first Phantom
(MDC)

OPPOSITE PAGE
In March 1978, two decades after making the first flight in a Phantom, Robert C Little shows that he can still do it. In a picture taken to commemorate the 20th anniversary of that first flight, a young-looking Bob Little mounts the five thousandth machine, F-4E-65MC Phantom 77-290 destined for the Turkish Air Force
(MDC)

BELOW
Believed to be the first picture ever taken of a Phantom in flight, reportedly taken by a General Electric employee who was 'hiding in the weeds near the runway.' Photo shows prototype F4H-1 Phantom 142259 with Robert C Little at the controls lifting off for its initial flight on 27 May 1958 (via MDC)

to provide pressurization for higher altitude operation. The next flight for pre-ferry shakedown purposes is expected by 7 June 1958.'

Flight testing continued. In 1958, the Phantom was a unique bird and sizeable crowds gathered to watch successful flights made by Little on June 18th (followed by another change of engines), June 19th (held below 25,000 ft (7,620 m) by overcast), and June 20th. Robert Little's experience culminated with the 23 June 1958 ferry flight which, with two stops en route, delivered the first Phantom from St Louis to Edwards AFB, Calif.

Testing went through the summer and the airplane was formally released from the company to the Navy for what it called 'Phase I evaluations.' At this point, considerable thought was being given to using the Phantom II to probe the outer reaches of fighter speed and altitude capability. Both for scientific reasons and for good public relations, the Navy wanted to show that it had a high-flying, fast airplane.

Phase I evaluations were conducted at Edwards through September and October 1958. Pilots from the Naval Air Test Center at Patuxent River made 43 flights. The F4H-1 was in competition with the Vought F8U-3 Crusader II for acceptance as the Navy's new Fleet Defense Aircraft. The F4H-1 emerged as the winner for several reasons, among them the two-place, twin-engine configuration.

Project TOP FLIGHT

By 1959, a second Phantom was in the air. But with plane number two, 142260, slated for engine development work it was anticipated that the first

machine would attempt an altitude record under the project now called TOP FLIGHT. The man who drew the assignment, Gerald 'Zeke' Huelsbeck of Hazelwood, Mo, now replaced Robert C Little as the most luminous star on the bent-wing bird's horizon.

Born 16 April 1928 in Neenah, Wisconsin, Huelsbeck had been a lieutenant (jg) in the Navy, flew 54 combat missions in the F2H-2 Banshee in Korea, and was a member of class number 11 in the Navy's Test Pilot School in 1954. 'Eased out of the Navy,' because of an independent streak, according to one McDonnell employee, he became a civilian to join the firm in 1955 as production test pilot. Two months later, he was promoted to experimental test pilot.

Married, with a sharpness of both wit and temper, Huelsbeck by mid-1959 had more experience in the F4H-1 at high speed and high altitude than any other flier.

Now, the scene had shifted from the manufacturer's airstrip in Middle America to the parched, searing heat of the California desert. By October 1959, eleven Phantom prototypes were flying. Still, 142259 was *the* Phantom. The TOP FLIGHT record attempt—to be made by Huelsbeck but with Commander Larry Flint as backup—was on everyone's mind. The Phantom—the 'winner' in pilot Mills' words—would now show its stuff.

Project TOP FLIGHT officially began with a flight on 15 September 1959. Fourteen experimental flights were made with increased RPMs and afterburner fuel flow, with no adverse effects.

When George S Mills went to the Goodrich plant in Ohio to be fitted for the pressure suit worn in early Phantoms, he had to wait in line behind Mercury astronaut John Glenn, whose suit was identical. Mills went on, as a McDonnell test pilot, to become the second man to fly the F-4 Phantom. Blurred aircraft in background is RF-101 Voodoo
(MDC)

By 15 September 1959 when this photo was taken at sunbaked Edwards AFB, Calif., the first Phantom (142259) was being readied by pilot Gerald 'Zeke' Huelsbeck for a dramatic attempt at a world altitude record. At this time the words TOP FLIGHT appeared on the aircraft and it wore bright red on the tail and wingtips, although there were apparently minor variations on this paint scheme throughout the period
(MDC)

The first F4H-1 Phantom (142259) with day-glo trim on
wings and tail and dummy Sparrow missiles in its under-
fuselage bays
(MDC)

OPPOSITE PAGE
*Thomas H Miller eventually became a combat commander
in Vietnam, a three-star lieutenant general, and the
highest-ranking naval/Marine aviator on active duty. At
about the time this photo was taken, Lt Col Miller set a
500-km closed-course speed record on 5 September 1960 in
F4H-1 Phantom 145311, the twelfth machine built—
although the early Phantom in this photo is a different
aircraft*
(MDC)

The Last Flight

Now, as a kind of final prelude to the altitude
record itself, Huelsbeck would take 142259 on a
maximum-altitude investigation with a gross
weight below that of previous efforts. Aft missiles,
lower radio antenna and tailhook were removed. A
routine take-off was made in satisfactory weather.

On this day, 21 October 1959, Zeke Huelsbeck
had logged 2,380 hours, 1,900 of them in jets
including 135 in the Phantom. The airplane itself,
142259, had now completed 295 flights for a total
of 254 hours, 32 minutes. And this day was to be
the last of mortal life for both man and machine.

Turning at Mach 2.15 over the California
desert, Huelsbeck reported 'something strange.'
He didn't know what. Position of the aircraft was

a few miles short of Mount Pinos, a frequently
used check point. No other sign of anxiety or
urgency was detected during Huelsbeck's radio
transmissions—but moments later, from radar
tracking, it became painfully evident that 142259
had crashed.

Although the pilot must never have known it,
the right engine aft access door ripped itself away
during flight. This caused a reduction of cooling in
the right engine nozzle, destruction of portions of
the engine nozzle by sheet heat, and an
impingement of engine exhaust gases upon the
lower portion of the center and aft fuselage. In
moments, there was a ripple effect, with damage to
hydraulic systems, radio communications, the

longitudinal feel system and the stabilator assembly. Afterward, investigators determined that the right engine aft access door tore itself away because locking bolts backed out due to improper fastening—but the accident investigation was hamstrung because the door was never found.

Two sentences in a company report tell of the demise of a fine test pilot: '*When ejection was attempted the canopy and ejection seat separated satisfactorily from the airplane, but altitude was too low for successfuly parachute deployment. The pilot was killed instantly upon impact with the ground.*'

At this point in history, 'zero-zero' ejection (at zero speed and/or zero altitude) was still a future hope. Early Phantoms were fitted with a McDonnell ejection seat which reflected the

technology of the time. The British-built Martin Baker ejection seat Mk 5 was to become standard on the Phantom. Its effectiveness would be greatly improved with the installation of the RAPEC III (rocket assisted personnel ejection catapult) replacing the original cartridge catapult. This new system, the Mk H7, provided ejection capability at ground level and zero knots airspeed. As a direct consequence of the 'higher ride' provided by RAPEC III, an improved 28-ft (8.5 m) personnel parachute would be installed with all block 40 Phantoms onward and retrofitted to all F-4C and F-4D models—but this lay ahead.

Ahead in the Phantom's future would be air-to-air combat kills in the Middle East and in North Vietnamese skies. Also ahead—more imminently—were a host of altitude and speed records so overwhelming that they rate as an achievement never equalled by a single aircraft type.

Project TOP FLIGHT went ahead and on 6 December 1959, Cdr Lawrence E Flint, Jr flew F4H-1 Phantom bureau number 142260, the second airplane, to a record 98,557 ft (30,000 m).

TOP LEFT
It is not generally known that two Phantom speed record airframes carried the nickname 'Sageburner.' The little-known first machine, seen here, was F4H-1 Phantom 145316, the seventeenth aircraft built, which crashed in a New Mexico speed run attempt on 18 May 1961, killing Cdr J L Felsman
(MDC)

BOTTOM LEFT
Cdr J L Felsman, at left, with Ensign R M Hite, has a week to live in this May 11th, 1961 photo with the little-known original 'Sageburner,' F4H-1 Phantom 145316 in the background. On 18 May 1961, Felsman was killed in a speed run in New Mexico in this aircraft
(MDC)

In the second 'Sageburner' aircraft, F4H-1 Phantom 145307, Lt Huntington Hardisty, at left with Lt Earl H 'Duke' DeEsch, set a speed record of 902.769 mph on 28 August 1961. Hardisty later commanded USS Kitty Hawk's *carrier air wing in 1972 Linebacker operations against North Vietnam*
(MDC)

On 22 November 1961, date of his 1,606-mph world's absolute speed record run in the number two F4H-1F Phantom (142260), Marine Corps Lt Col Robert B Robinson climbs aboard. The speed run was called Operation Skyburner. Robinson is retired in the St Louis area today

A world air speed record for a 100-km course was established on 25 September 1960, when Cdr John Franklin (Jeff) Davis reached 1,390.21 mph (2,238 km/h), apparently in Phantom 143389, the fourth machine built.

Another world air speed record, for a 500-km closed course of 1,216.78 mph (1,958 km/h) was accomplished 5 September 1960 by Lt Col Thomas H Miller of the Marine Corps in Phantom number 145311, the twelfth machine built.

Then came a tragedy, during an attempt to set a speed record at extremely low level. It is a little-known fact of Phantom lore that *two* speed-record aircraft carried the nickname 'Sageburner,' the first being 145316, the seventeenth Phantom built. On 18 May 1961, at the speed range at Kirtland AFB, New Mexico, Cdr J L Felsman was going for the absolute speed record in 145316 when pitch dampener failure led to pilot induced oscillation, causing the Phantom to break apart and explode in a fiery, spectacular crash which cost Felsman's life. At the time, 145316 was

carrying a one-of-a-kind centreline instrumentation pod and was marked with the insignia of Kirtland's Naval Weapons Experiment Facility (NWEF).

In the second attempt under Project Sageburner, on 28 August 1961, Lt Huntington Hardisty set a speed record of 902.769 mph (1,452 km/h) in F4H-1 Phantom 145307, the eighth machine built, which is now in storage for the National Air Museum in Washington, DC. Hardisty made the flight at 125 ft of altitude, still breathtakingly low—but never again would such a speed run be tried 'on the deck.' Hardisty later commanded a carrier air wing in combat operations against North Vietnam in 1972.

In Project Skyburner on 22 November 1961, Lt Col Robert B Robinson of the Marine Corps reached a new world absolute speed record in F4H-1F, as the craft had now been redesignated, number 142260, again the second Phantom built.

In 1962, in Project High Jump, no less than eight separate altitude records were achieved by the F4H-1 Phantom!

Ahead lay three decades of Phantom operations. But it all began with the machine which flew only from 27 May 1958 until 21 October 1959, the little-praised first of all Phantoms—the prototype machine which had a brief but brave life and which began it all.

Chapter 2
To The Fleet, The Corps, The War
Introduction to Navy and Marine Service

Elder, Spencer, O'Rourke, Lake. These and others were to have the distinction of being first in Phantoms, a feat they would treasure for a lifetime. Their squadrons would be named with those offbeat and macabre appellations unique to American naval aviation—the Be-Devilers, the Aardvarks, the Grim Reapers.

Beginning almost with the first flight tests of the Phantom in May 1958, an exhaustive flight development programme was embarked upon to prove out all aspects of the basic design and to evaluate changes that were found necessary. For example, some 75 flights by company pilots were required to show the airplane capable of satisfactory operation at speeds and altitudes required for the first Navy Primary Evaluation (NPE). The NPE was undertaken in September 1958 by eight pilots at the Naval Air Test Center (NATC), Patuxent River, Maryland headed by Capt R M Elder. 'We were really wringing the new bird out,' recalls one of Elder's enlisted technicians. 'We put it through every conceivable stress. It impressed us as one sturdy flying machine.'

Carrier suitability trials were conducted with the sixth F4H-1 (143391), lavish in red trim, aboard the 78,700-ton USS *Independence* (CVA-62) off the Atlantic coast, 15–20 February 1960. The Phantom's sturdiness and suitability seemed apparent, even when Lt Cdr Paul E Spencer operated from *Independence*'s angled deck with dummy bombs simulating heavy centreline ordnance. Some subsequent flights were made by Cdr Larry Flint, back-up pilot who had set the 98,557-ft (30,000 m) altitude mark the previous December. 18 catapult launches were made in all. Few major obstacles were encountered.

The second set of carrier trials was made aboard USS *Intrepid* (CV-11), a much smaller carrier displacing 41,900 tons when fully provisioned. These trials, held 25–7 April included more than 20 catapults and arrested landings.

A young sailor aboard *Intrepid* saved the precious F4H-1 from damage which could have been serious enough to delay the tests. Seaman Donald S Pickard was admiring the machine being removed from *Intrepid*'s narrow elevator below decks when he noticed that its tail was about to collide with an overhead obstruction. Just in time, Pickard persuaded deck handlers to raise the Phantom into a nose-high attitude to clear the obstacle. 'It was a tight squeak,' says Pickard who, in this narrative, will reappear over Hanoi.

Aboard *Intrepid*, a minor but troublesome problem arose when the arresting hook skipped upon touching the deck. Minor changes in the design quickly solved this. During the carrier tests, waveoffs were flown on one engine without using afterburner—never to become recommended practice. The engines demonstrated that they could be accelerated from the approach power setting to full thrust within one second.

TOP RIGHT
Cdr Paul Spencer, later to become the first man to make 100 carrier landings in a Phantom, prepares for launch in the sixth F4H-1 Phantom (143391) during shipboard qualifications off the Atlantic coast in April 1960 (MDC)

Two key Phantom figures. Cdr Lawrence E Flint, Jr, at left, set an altitude record in the F4H-1. Cdr Gerald O'Rourke headed Detachment A of the 'Grim Reapers' of VF-101 on the east coast and helped create the first Replacement Air Group, or RAG, units. On 14 April 1961, Flint and O'Rourke are located in front of an F4H-1 Phantom 'status' board in the ops room of the first west coast squadron, the 'Pacemakers' of VF-121 at NAS Miramar, California (US Navy)

Spencer was optimistic. 'The F4H is a big airplane. It is twice the weight of the F11F (Grumman Tiger) and nearly three times the weight of the A4D (Douglas Skyhawk). Yet with all of this bulk it handles better than any of our modern Navy fighters.

'Former single-engine pilots will find the responsiveness of the two J79 engines somewhat close to sensational,' added Spencer, who had flown 35 types of aircraft.

Sensational was the right word. Capt Norman D Campbell came to the Phantom from the attack community, having flown the AD-6 Skyraider and A4D-1 Skyhawk. Like many attack pilots, accustomed to violent maneuvering and low-level action, he was impressed with the Phantom's enormous power on afterburner. But, he observes, many pilots failed to notice that being on burner ate up fuel. 'When we flew the aircraft with both burners, its use of fuel jumped from 5,000 lb (2,260 lit) per hour to 17,000 lb (7,700 kg). An over-zealous pilot could easily find himself without enough fuel to carry out his assigned mission.'

Early contracts had resulted in construction of 47 F4H-1 aircraft, redesignated F4H-1F in March 1961, and again redesignated F-4A with the major changes in nomenclature of the following year. With two further firm contracts signed 23 September 1959 and 1 August 1960 for 72 aircraft each, known initially as the F4H-1 and later as the F-4B, and with other development work proceeding rapidly, no one had seriously doubted that the Phantom would be able to operate from carrier decks. Very possibly, less thought had been given to finding the people to do it, particularly in the back seat. In 1959–61, no front-line Navy fighter carried a second crewman, and not enough work had been done in recruiting ROs (radar operators) who, early in the Phantom's life, would be re-christened RIOs (radar intercept officers).

In the Pentagon, men sought to anticipate the shortage of RIOs and other teething problems. As early as mid-1959, Cdr Harry Gibbs and Lt Col Thomas H Miller were assigned as 'class desk officers' at the Bureau of Naval Weapons (the former Bureau of Aeronautics) in the Pentagon, planning to cope with operational requirements. The presence of Miller was a measure of the Marine Corps' feeling of immediacy towards the Phantom. Miller was a dark-haired, deliberate, and deceptively mild man, a ham radio enthusiast who had set the 1,216 mph (1,958 km/h) closed-course speed record that September, who would command Marine Air in South Vietnam at the beginning and would ultimately wear the three stars of a lieutenant general on his shoulders as the 'Gray Eagle,' the senior among all active naval/Marine aviators. His homey expression and subdued style disguised a firmness which could be detected only in the riveting gaze of his brown eyes. He wanted Marines driving Phantoms and he wanted it now.

Normally land-based, but charged with the capability to operate from carriers, Marine aviators had had a long history of receiving first-line aircraft only long after their Navy brethren. The Marines wanted the Phantom right away. Gibbs was soon replaced by Cdr Jeff Davis, and Davis and Miller functioned as a two-man team on Phantom planning until mid-1961 when they were replaced by Cdr Edward L (Whitey) Feightner and Lt Col Robert B Robinson, another Marine record holder. The 'Black Knights' of VMF(AW)-314, the first Marine squadron to be formed at El Toro, near San Diego, California, were gearing up for delivery of the new aircraft as early as mid-1961, not far behind the first Navy units.

Shore Duty: The RAGs and the RIOs

In late 1959, Lt Cdr Gerald G O'Rourke went to Key West, on the tip of Florida, to begin forming the first F4H-1 RAG units, the 'replacement air group' squadrons which would work up the Phantom as a combat-ready, Fleet service aircraft. O'Rourke was chosen to help put together the first Phantom workups because of his advocacy of two-seat fighter aircraft and because of his experience in F3D Skyknights, including combat operations in Korea with the 'Flying Nightmares' of VMF(N)-513, a Marine night-fighter squadron which would shortly become part of the Phantom story.

The RAGs were the first Phantom squadrons. On the east coast, to support the Atlantic Fleet, was VF-101, the 'Grim Reapers,' at Key West with its small Detachment A at NAS Oceana, Virginia, in the same tidewater area where carriers were home-ported. The squadron's aircraft had an AD tailcode. (East coast/Atlantic squadrons have codes beginning with A; west coast/Pacific squadrons codes beginning with N; all of the aircraft aboard a single carrier, that is, all of the machines in the same carrier air wing, have the same two-letter code). On the west coast, supporting the Pacific Fleet, was VF-121, 'the Pacemakers' at NAS Miramar, California with an NJ tailcode. VF-121 received its first Phantom (148256) at Miramar on 30 December 1960. The east coast squadron was not far behind.

O'Rourke's first problem was, where to get RIOs? In the Pentagon, Lt Col Miller was secretly pleased that the Marine Corps still operated the two-seat F3D Skyknight and had a cadre of RIO candidates available. Not so, the Navy. Radar intercept officers were an almost non-existent breed in the single-seat Navy of 1960. Several Navy officers were chosen and received RIO training at James Connally AFB, Texas, but they needed a machine to fly while Phantoms were still sparse. O'Rourke scurried around the country 'scrounging up' recently retired Skyknights for them to fly. On one occasion, he halted a F3D being towed by tractor out through the gate at Litchfield Park, Arizona, destined to be placed on outdoor 'gate guardian' display somewhere, because he needed the plane for parts.

O'Rourke's F3D Skyknights, with jury-rigged radar that earned them the new designation F3D-2T-2, began 'bringing up' RIOs with Detachment A of the RAG squadron, VF-101's 'Grim Reapers,' at Oceana. An enterprising officer combined an F3D cockpit with an F3H Demon radar to create an 'obnoxious-looking'—says O'Rourke—device which was against regulations and unplanned, but used effectively at Oceana. Because O'Rourke's F3Ds had been designed for JP-3 fuel, which was no longer readily suppliable, he and his fellow officers had to search for supplies of Avtur which was more expensive than any standard fuel then in use. At one point, a maintenance man decreed that all F3Ds would have to be grounded because it was costing too much to fly them. He was overruled. Throughout 1960, aircrews in F3Ds practiced two-seat intercept tactics using F9F-8T Cougars as targets.

Early Phantoms were pitted in mock combat against the US Air Force's Convair F-106 Delta Darts, then still fairly new. Aggressive, goal-oriented Cdr Julian S Lake wanted to prove his new mount against the Air Force's best and managed to outfight them in most regimes. This

may have sparked the initial Air Force interest in what was, until then, a Navy aircraft.

The first production F4H-1, quickly to be redubbed the F-4B, made its first flight on 25 March 1961, and the first two operational sea squadrons began receiving their aircraft in July. These were VF-74, the 'Be-Devilers,' under Lake on the east coast and VF-114, the 'Aardvarks,' under Cdr Joseph J Konzen on the west. Lake's squadron completed carrier qualifications on the USS *Saratoga* (CVA-60) in October.

The 'Be-Devilers' originally underwent their Phantom training with VF-101 Det A at Oceana, taking advantage of some of O'Rourke's innovations with air intercept tactics. When VF-74 received its own Phantoms, the squadron immediately joined a project devised by the Navy to bring its swift new interceptor to the public's attention, *Project Lana*.

To celebrate the 50th anniversary of Naval Aviation, the Navy decided to enter four of its new Phantoms in the 1961 Bendix Trophy Race to break the existing Los Angeles to New York speed

Project Lana, marking the 50th anniversary of naval aviation on 24 May 1961, sent five F4H-1F Phantoms on a speed dash across the United States from Ontario, California to Floyd Bennett Field in New York. Four days before the speed run, F4H-1 Phantom 148268, coded AD-184, of the 'Grim Reapers' of Detachment A squadron VF-101 is serviced at Ontario. Fuselage stripe was painted for the Lana event, which resulted in 2445.9 statute miles being covered in two hours 48 minutes, at an average speed of 869 mph
(US Navy)

record, three hours and seven minutes, set by a US Air Force RF-101 Voodoo in 1957. Cdr Lake and his RIO, Lt (jg) E A Cowart, along with three other F4H crews from VF-101 and VF-121 were chosen as participants in the *Project Lana* speed effort.

Lake and Cowart launched from Ontario International Airport near Los Angeles on the morning of 24 May 1961. Three hours and three minutes later, after two mid-air refuellings from Douglas A3D Skywarriors—still a new exercise for the Phantom—Lake flashed by the tower at Floyd Bennett Field in New York, cutting four minutes off the previous record. His triumph was short-lived, however, for less than seven minutes later *Lana Two* piloted by Lt Cdr Scott Lamoreaux and Lt T J Johnson completed the race in 2 hours, 27 minutes, breaking Lake's record. They were in turn bested by the ultimate winners of the race, *Lana Three*, piloted by Lt Richard F Gordon and Lt (jg) Bobbie R Young of VF-121, whose record-breaking time was 2 hours 24 minutes. In less than fifteen minutes, the old record had been beaten three times by Phantoms.

Sea Duty: The First Carrier Squadrons

With VF-74's 'Be-Devilers' going aboard *Saratoga* in the Atlantic and VF-114's 'Aardvarks' embarking on *Kitty Hawk* (CVA-63) in the Pacific, it was only a matter of time before another milestone would be achieved, namely the first pilot to make 100 arrested landings in the Phantom. The original carrier qualifications pilot who now became VF-74's second skipper in its Phantom era, Cdr Paul E Spencer, achieved this 'centurion' mark just after the Be-Devilers shifted to *Forrestal* (CVA-59) for a Mediterranean cruise in 1962.

The powerful Phantom was received well. Carriers traditionally embarked with two fighter squadrons, and at this juncture several carriers

*From this direction, most models of the F-4 Phantom look about the same. This April 1962 view of a Phantom with a full load of ordnance is believed to depict the US Navy's F4H-1F 145310, which became redesignated F-4A a few months later
(MDC)*

were at sea with one squadron of Phantoms, one of F-8 Crusaders. Competition between the two was fierce. The Crusader was a highly successful single-seat, single-engine fighter and highly manoeuvrable in a fight. Phantom pilots, in mock contests with the F-8, may never have foreseen that they were gaining experience they would need against the MiG-21. Their airplane had been designed to fight, even if few saw it yet as more than an interceptor, and fight it would in the period of history immediately ahead.

The 'Fighting Falcons' of VF-96 became the second operational Pacific squadron (after VF-114), beginning to 'work up' in November 1961 and becoming fully operational in June 1962. This squadron's tailcode was NG. VF-96, which would produce two aces over North Vietnam a decade later, was first to fly the Phantom in already-troubled Southeast Asia climes, while aboard *Ranger* (CVA-61) in a cruise which lasted from 9 November 1962 to 14 June 1963. With John F Kennedy in the White House and American forces in South Vietnam numbering a mere 5,000, the Phantom crews of VF-96 could only guess what awaited them.

In the Atlantic, the second east coast squadron to become operational in the F4H Phantom (after VF-74) was VF-102, nicknamed the 'Diamondbacks' and commanded by O'Rourke. Historian Walter A Trimborn points out that the 'Diamondbacks' began working up with the east coast RAG (VF-101 Det A) as early as 15 September 1961 with initial training completed by December 15. After field carrier landing practices, VF-102 went aboard *Independence* (CVA-62) on 18 January 1962 for crew members' carrier qualifications, returning to landbased operations at Oceana on 26 January. The 'Diamondbacks,' wearing an AF tailcode, then embarked on the shakedown cruise of the newly commissioned nuclear-powered *Enterprise* (CVAN-65). Twelve VF-102 Phantoms took off from Oceana on 14 February 1962 with their destination *Enterprise*, operating in the Carribean and Guantanamo Bay some 1,340 miles (2,157 km/h) away. One of the pilots on this trip was Lt (jg) Bruce McCandless, later to be famous as an astronaut who made the first untethered 'walk' from the space shuttle *Challenger*.

Enterprise completed her shakedown training on 5 April and returned to Norfolk on 8 April. During June 1962, VF-102 officially joined the air wing aboard *Enterprise*. Accompanied by *Forrestal*, carrying the Be-Devilers of VF-74, *Enterprise* left Norfolk on 3 August 1962 for her first deployment in the Mediterranean.

The men were 'up' about their new aircraft but not every experience was happy. Even with a tried and tested machine, and even in peacetime, life aboard a carrier is fraught with peril. On 9 March

1963, because of a catapult failure, VF-102's O'Rourke found himself under water, upside-down, strapped inside a fast-sinking Phantom with a 60,000-ton aircraft carrier passing over him. O'Rourke escaped. His RIO, Lt James Philo, did not. In another incident, a VF-74 pilot flew into wavecaps on launch, gained a few feet of altitude for a few seconds, and instructed his RIO to eject. This time, the back-seater survived. The pilot did not.

Yet another Navy squadron achieved readiness in the F4H-1 Phantom in the east coast/Atlantic region at an early date. VF-41, known as the 'Black Aces,' completed its initial training in the Phantom in March 1962 to become the third operational Phantom squadron in the Atlantic Fleet aboard the *Independence* (CVA-62).

VF-41, with fourteen aircraft and seventeen pilot/RIO crews—for it was indeed the custom, by now, for the two-man teams to stay together as cohesive crews—deployed for temporary duty to NAS Key West, Florida on 9 October 1962 to strengthen the air defence of the Southeastern United States during the Cuban missile crisis. They were under the operational control of the North American Air Defense Command (NORAD) between 22 October and 22 November—the critical period when President Kennedy acted firmly and Nikita Khruschev 'blinked.' During this period, VF-41's 'Black Aces' achieved a tempo of air operations which was approximately three times the normal Phantom flying rate.

The Cuban missile crisis came and went without the F-4B Phantom being tested in battle although, as will shortly be related, Castro's MiG-17s nearly brushed with the Phantom. In Southeast Asia, it would be different. Meanwhile, as the decade grew older, the US Air Force began to show interest in the Phantom—the machine it would first call the F-110A, then the F-4C. But first, the urgency with which the United States Marine Corps regarded the new airplane had to be confronted.

The Corps and the War

The first Marine to fly a Phantom was Lt Col Robert J Barbour, a crew-cut, bulky, stern-faced man symbolic of the Corps' toughness: He'd survived a near-fatal 1943 crash in an SNJ trainer to fly every fighter in Corps inventory from the F4U Corsair to the F3D Skyknight, and to win battle decorations in the 1950–3 Korean conflict. As a test pilot under Elder at Patuxent, on 6 October 1959, he went aloft in the number three machine (143388). That aircraft is the oldest surviving Phantom today, rotting outdoors at the US Marine Corps Museum in Quantico, Virginia. Barbour, who would figure later in the Phantom story, was enthralled with the new airplane.

INSET
A Marine in a new war and a future MiG killer, W/O John D Cummings leans on the Zuni pod of F-4B Phantom 151443 of the 'Gray Ghosts' of VMFA-531 at Da Nang in May 1965. Cummings has been a radar intercept officer (RIO) since 1962. On 11 September 1972, together with Maj 'Bear' Lasseter (since deceased), his was the only Marine Phantom crew to shoot down a MiG while flying a Marine Corps aircraft. In 1980, while commanding the 'Warlords' of VMFA-451, Cummings became the first RIO and the first Marine to exceed 4,000 flight hours in the Phantom
(Lt Col John D Cummings)

The 'Black Knights' of Marine squadron VMFA-314 operated Phantoms from 1962 to 1984, before their familiar VW tail-code was painted on the F/A-18 Hornet. F-4N-41-MC Phantom 153011, coded VW-12, is seen at NAS Alameda, California on 16 May 1982
(Tom Chee)

Lt Col Thomas H Miller was originally slated to command the first Marine Corps squadron at MCAS El Toro, near San Diego, California, forming in 1962. This was VMF(AW)-314, the 'Black Knights.' Due to some unfortunate events involving the death of his executive officer to-be and because he could not arrive before July of that year, it was decided that Lt Col Barbour would take command of VMF(AW)-314. Miller would then take the second west coast Marine squadron late in 1962. Meanwhile, the first east coast squadron, VMF(AW)-531, under Lt Col Robert F Foxworth, would form at MCAS Beaufort, South Carolina in June or July 1962.

Years later, to the frustrated historian, it is almost impossible to sort out a question as simple as, which Marine Corps squadron received the Phantom first? Says Lt Col John D Cummings, a remarkably small man with a ready grin, who would later become a MiG killer and the world's most experienced Phantom back-seater: 'We should set the record straight. Although VMF(AW)-314 had the most publicity, those of us in '531 have no doubts that we were really the first (and only) F-4 squadron.' Says Miller: 'As it worked out, '314 commenced getting its aircraft in May and June 1962 and '531 in June and July.'

Says Barbour: 'Tom Miller was right, Cummings wrong; 314 was first . . .'

Cummings and his fellow Marines in the 'Gray Ghosts' of VMF(AW)-531 started transition training in the F4H-1 Phantom at Oceana on 31 July 1962. Elaine Collins, whose husband Col George Collins was about to hand over command of the squadron, walked around Cherry Point and found squadron personnel painting the letters 'EC' on one of the aircraft. Her husband told Elaine that he intended to put her initials on all of the squadron aircraft so that he would always be reminded of her! Only months later did Elaine Collins learn that EC was the standard Marine tailcode for the squadron and had no connection with her name! Meanwhile, after a two-week stint during which Maj Orie E Cory was temporarily in charge, command of VMF(AW)-531 passed to Lt Col Robert F Foxworth, a rugged career Marine

Among the earliest photos of a Marine Corps Phantom on a carrier, this unpublished view supplied by British exchange officer Sqn Ldr Ian Hamilton shows the 'Gray Ghosts' of VMFA-531 caught up in the squadron's CARQUALs (carrier qualifications) on Forrestal (CVA-59) in March 1964. F-4B-11-MC Phantom 149465, coded EC-14, has just landed on the carrier's angled deck and is taxying in the 'full flaps' position (US Marine Corps, VMCJ-2)

Her Majesty's men in a Marine mount. The first British Royal Air Force exchange officers serving with the 'Gray Ghosts' of VMFA-531, Flt Lt James Sawyer (left) and Sqn Ldr Ian B Hamilton aboard the USS Forrestal *(CVA-59) in the Atlantic, March 1964 (US Marine Corps)*

RIGHT
Lt Col Robert F Foxworth took command of Marine squadron VMF(AW)-531 at Cherry Point, NC in July 1962, just as the squadron was transitioning into F-4s (US Marine Corps)

who looked like a recruiting poster. Foxworth had made his own first flight in an F4H-1 Phantom (149460) on 6 July 1962 at Oceana.

Cooperation between the Navy and Marine Corps enabled Marine maintenance and flight crews to train with the east and west coast Navy RAGs—by now very experienced. Thus, the Navy trained VMFA-314 and VMFA-531. The 'VMF(AW)' designation, indicating all-weather, was deemed unnecessary and replaced on 1 August 1963 by VMFA, which added the attack function and ended the period when the Phantom could be considered solely an interceptor.

VMFA-531 on the east coast seems to have the distinction of being the first Marine squadron to experience a bailout. It was also the first to include British officers in exchange tours. On 2 November 1962, squadron commander Foxworth welcomed Sqn Ldr Ian B Hamilton of the Royal Air Force and explained, 'I'll tell you more about us just after this flight.' Foxworth went aloft in an F-4B Phantom (149462) with Captain Dan Benn as his rear-seater. 30 miles (48 km) north of Cherry Point at about 4,000 ft (1,220 m), he experienced a double generator failure. This was followed by a control system malfunction when the 'pop-out'

ram air turbine (RAT) generator failed to perform as advertised. There was no choice but to punch out.

Since the back-seater always leaves the aircraft first, Benn ejected and managed to land in a clearing near a country road. Foxworth broke a leg on landing and had to wait for a helicopter to pick him up. Benn, although not required to, was wearing the futuristic full pressure suit just for the practice of wearing one; he looked like a man from Mars. Since he was not injured, he tucked his big helmet under his arm and set off down the country road looking for a telephone. Soon he spotted a

All Marine squadrons have permanently-assigned two-letter tail codes. The last commander of the 'Gray Ghosts' of VMFA-531 just before the Phantom era in July 1962, Col George Collins, told his wife Elaine that he was going to paint her initials on the tails of all squadron aircraft. Eleven years later, the markings remained little changed, as seen in this 23 September 1973 photo of F-4B-13-MC Phantom (150478) at NAS North Island, California. 150478 survived to be converted under a service life extension program (SLEP) to F-4N-23-MC (James T Sullivan)

small farmhouse and knocked on the front door. A surprised black woman opened the door and, on seeing Dan Benn in the pressure suit, gawked in disbelief. 'Good morning, lady,' said Benn. 'I wonder if you can tell me where I am.' Jaw open, she stammered, 'Why why man, you you in the United States of America!'

The situation was different when Tom Miller organized the third Marine squadron (and second on the west coast), the 'Flying Nightmares' of VMFA-513, in October 1962. The one-time Korean War Skyknight squadron would now fly the single-seat Douglas F-6A Skyray (formerly F4D-1, and inevitably called the Ford) until Phantom deliveries could commence in early 1963.

Until Miller worked up 513, the only Marine pilots permitted in the F-4 were experienced flyers serving at least their second tour after qualifying in some other aircraft type. Miller was asked if he would be willing to take men straight out of flight school and make them F-4 pilots. He agreed that he could, provided he was able to set up a special flight training syllabus to prepare new pilots for the Phantom. Additionally, Miller was permitted to arrange from mutual training with the Navy's RAG squadron for his first-tour pilots in return for lending Marine RIOs to the RAG as instructors. Says Miller of the problem O'Rourke faced earlier: 'The Navy was extremely short of experienced radar intercept officers because they had done away with this requirement a long time before whereas the Marine Corps had continued to operate the two-seat F3D nightfighter.' It was beginning to sound like a broken record.

Meanwhile, whilst awaiting its blooding at the Gulf of Tonkin in 1964, the F-4B Phantom nearly had a go at Fidel Castro. As a back-seater from the 'Gray Ghosts' of Marine squadron VMFA-531 puts it:

'Although we'd just begun to operate our planes in October 1962 when the Cuban missile crisis occurred, our CO (Foxworth) was chomping at the bit to get us into action. He succeeded but we were too late. After the crisis, in February 1963, we were sent to Key West to strip alert duty for six months. We kept two aircraft on five-minute alert and two on fifteen minute alert throughout the entire deployment. This was the greatest thing that could have happened to a young flier because the Key West 'hot pad' was very busy at that time. I made over 50 actual scrambles, each to intercept (usually a lost Mexican airliner) almost always at night or in bad weather. Because of our alert status, '531 had good support for parts, fuel and that sort of neat stuff so all of us got a lot of flight time and intercepts early in our careers. When we weren't on alert we flew training missions . . .

'While at Key West, we found that the ancient MiG-17 might be a formidable machine under the right (or wrong) conditions. It seems that the

Cuban MiGs had strafed a fishing boat about 50 miles south of Key West and some of our planes were scrambled to investigate. After arriving on the scene our Phantoms and Fidel's MiGs jockeyed for position and it soon became apparent that the MiG had the shorter turn radius. As a MiG rolled in behind one of our planes the RIO said, 'You'd better do some of that pilot shit 'cause we're losing.' That phrase became synonymous with manoeuvring the airplane in that squadron . . .'

To shift the scene again, back to VMFA-513, Tom Miller's background as a 'class desk officer' at the Pentagon enabled him to recruit the most experienced officers and enlisted men in the Corps. War clouds were gathering. As Miller put it, 'This paid off and '513 established a superb record of accomplishments throughout the squadron's tour, including its combat tour in South Vietnam in 1965.' In 1964, VMFA-513 made the first air-to-air kill of the Beech AGM-64 (formerly KD-2B) Katybird supersonic drone (which was carried and dropped by the Phantom), using Sidewinders at Point Mugu, California. Other records for 'most missiles fired' were toted up by the squadron as its men worked up with the heat-seeking Sidewinder and the semi-homing Sparrow. In April 1964, with RIO Capt Ronald C Kropp in the back seat, Miller flew the F-4B farther than it had ever been flown without refuelling or stopping, a 3-hour, 40-

1/Lts Robert Pennell and Kevin Grennan of the 'Flying Nightmares' of Marine squadron VMFA-513 did everything right when their F-4B Phantom (150433) lost an engine on a night flight in bad weather on 28 January 1964—and lived. The crew is seen examining the Phantom from which they ejected on landing approach at MCAS El Toro, California (US Marine Corps)

RIGHT
May 1963 view over Missouri is posed to illustrate the three US services which have ordered the Phantom (top to bottom): US Air Force, Navy and Marine Corps. All three machines are F-4B model

minute dash from El Toro to Cherry Point spanning 2,080 nm (3,850 km).

Though the twin J79-powered F-4B was an intricate machine, ground crews praised its ease of access and the comprehensive way McDonnell had developed methods for repair and upkeep. Accidents occurred at a rate far lower than for most newly introduced types. Marines were especially pleased at their high combat readiness level and low incidence of mishaps. But brake failures were a 'fluke' problem for a brief time and chilling experiences did occur.

At El Toro on 28 January 1964, 1/Lts Robert Pennell and Kevin Grennan of VMFA-513 took off for a night flight in very poor weather. Shortly after take-off and while still very heavy with fuel, they lost electrical power on one engine. Under these conditions, directions called for the pilot to

shut that engine down. Pennell did so, but it put him in a very heavy condition with only one engine for a landing under extremely difficult weather conditions. With considerable skill, Pennell handled the aircraft well until he reached the final phase of his approach when he lowered his flaps and landing gear. Under the extreme pressure of the situation at night, the aircraft got too slow and started sinking more rapidly than he could recover the required airspeed with the maximum power that he had available with the one engine. The Phantom is not supposed to be flown on one engine, not ever. When he realized that the aircraft was going out of control at very low altitude, Pennell instructed the RIO to bail out and followed suit. In early Phantoms, the back-seater's departure sometimes created a vacuum which held the front-seat pilot's canopy firmly in place despite all efforts to jettison it, a condition later corrected with explosive bolts on the front canopy but highly dangerous until then because the canopy *must* be jettisoned before a bailout can take place. This time, everything worked right and the aircraft hit in a special path that had been left clear of houses by a court decision which followed a bitter court trial—a decision real estate people are still trying to reverse today. Pennell's aircraft piled up nose-high in grass and low scrub trees—and burned. They walked away shaken and sobered. Their machine (150433) was 'write-off,' uneconomical to repair. 'It was not a good day,' a witness recalls.

Marine Phantoms deployed to Atsugi, Japan with Barbour's 'Black Knights' of VMFA-314 in April 1963, on a long El Toro–Hawaii–Wake Island–Atsugi jump refuelled by Lockheed KC-130Fs. VMFA-531 followed in August, VMFA-513 in October. President Kennedy would be assassinated and the Phantom bloodied in the Gulf of Tonkin air strikes before a fourth Marine squadron, VMFA-542, would join the others as part of Marine Aircraft Group 11 (MAG 11) in August 1965.

Tom Miller turned over command of '513 to Lt Col Walt Stewart in order to become commanding officer of MAG-11 (Forward) at a base new to the Corps' lexicon—Da Nang. In early 1965, the fiction was fast falling apart that Marines were in Vietnam only to protect US bases and not to participate in combat. Lyndon B Johnson's big build-up was under way. The Phantom was at war.

The Gulf of Tonkin

In the early 1960s as the Phantom spread its wings—the 'Ghostriders' of VF-142 and 'Pukin Dogs' of VF-143 went aboard *Constellation* (CVA-64) in the Western Pacific as Phantom squadrons multiplied—the slow but gradual heightening of involvement in Southeast Asia was accompanied by debate over bombing North Vietnam, which was supplying guerillas in the south. In his 1964 presidential campaign against Lyndon B Johnson, Senator Barry Goldwater favoured striking targets in the North to choke off the flow of supplies.

The inescapable provocation came on the night of 2–3 August 1964, when North Vietnamese torpedo boats attacked the 7th Fleet destroyers *Maddox* and *C Turner Joy* in international waters in the Gulf of Tonkin. *Maddox* was undamaged and fended off the attackers with the help of four F-8 Crusaders from the carrier *Ticonderoga* (CVA-14). A second clash followed. The Pentagon's Joint Chiefs of Staff decided that the United States must 'clobber' the attackers. Johnson supported this gut reaction and ordered retaliation.

Navy planes from *Ticonderoga* and *Constellation* on 4–5 August bombed North Vietnamese coastal bases, patrol boats, and an oil storage dump. In the 5-hour raid along 100 miles (160 km) of coastline, two attack aircraft were shot down—one man captured, one killed. Phantoms of VF-142 and VF-143 flew top cover. Though there have been some reports of a Phantom being damaged by ground fire that day, this appears not to have been the case. As Cdr F T Brown, skipper of VF-143 put it, 'No damage was documented to any F-4s that day. The Navy used its F-4s strictly in the air-to-air role, that is, BARCAP, escort, and so on. Thus, the F-4s had the advantage of missing the fun of the air-to-mud missions where the anti-aircraft fire was murderous . . .' On the same cruise, an F-4B Phantom (151402) of VF-142 was lost in an accident due to a stall on 13 November 1964—apparently the very first Phantom casualty in the Southeast Asia conflict—but on the day of the famous Gulf of Tonkin air strikes, Phantoms were unchallenged, undamaged.

Chapter 3
Rolling Thunder
The Air Force and the Out-Country War

The ease with which the US Air Force assimilated a *Navy* aircraft was astonishing.

'There was nothing else on the horizon,' acknowledges Col Alfred H Uhalt, Jr, who went to NAS Oceana, Virginia in October 1961 to check out the new bird and whose logbook shows flights in F4H-1 (later F-4B) aircraft 148366, 370, 373, 374 and 382. If Uhalt was not the first US Air Force pilot to fly the Phantom, he was first to submit the aircraft to rigorous 'shaking down' in varying performance regimes.

By March 1962, F-4B Phantoms 149405 and 149406 were flying at Edwards AFB, California. Both were Navy machines in Air Force markings with the unmistakable winged-sword badge of the Tactical Air Command painted in oversize on the fin. 149405 briefly had the designation F-110A painted on the nose. Uhalt and his fellow airmen thought they were receiving a plane called the F-110A Spectre.

Swallowing its pride about accepting a carrier-based *naval* design, the Air Force moved quickly. The service rushed Navy F-4Bs into its own colours for early operational use and—to keep the St Louis production line running—allowed its F-4Cs to be manufactured with a small infrared (IR) probe housing beneath the radome, even though the Navy's IR device was never installed on Air Force machine. With the changes in military designations effected on 18 September 1962, the F-110A became the F-4C and the Spectre name was discarded.

'We loved the Phantom from the start,' says Col Kenneth W Cordier who, as a new lieutenant, went to MacDill AFB near Tampa Bay in Florida to work up in the Air Force's F-4Bs and F-4Cs. So quickly was the Air Force building up its Phantom force that, in 1963–64, MacDill was in the extraordinary situation of having *two* Tactical

Headquarters building of the 8th Tactical Fighter Wing's 'Wolfpack' with the slogan 'Ye Who Passeth through These Portals Stand Tall' and the wing's MiG kills posted as red stars beneath the sign

Fighter Wings in domicile, the 12 TFW (its squadrons being the 555, 556 and 557 TFS) and the 15 TFW (comprising the 45, 46 and 47 TFS). When the Phantom replaced the Republic F-84F Thunderstreak with the 12 TFW under Col Harold M McClelland on 5 December 1963, the *Tampa Times* reported that, 'probably never again will the Air Force buy another one-seater fighter plane . . .' A spokesman for the wing added, 'This plane is outstanding. It's a fantastic hunk of machine. Going from the F-84F to the F-4C is like going from a Model T to a Mercedes-Benz . . .'

Twenty-nine borrowed Navy F-4Bs, given Air Force serial numbers but eventually returned to the Fleet, were quickly joined by F-4Cs which

retained the paint scheme of light gull gray on
upper surfaces and white underneath and on
control surfaces. The 555 TFS, the 'Triple Nickel'
squadron—with F-4C airframe 63-7555 as its
commander's mount long before matching serials
with unit names became common practice—was
deployed to Kadena AB, Okinawa in 1964. In
early 1965, the 45 TFS took up temporary station
in a tension-ridden zone, at Ubon, Thailand.
Before long, Uhalt and Cordier would be in
combat in Vietnam.

The photo reconnaissance variant of the
Phantom came along with the haste that
characterized everything happening in the early
and mid-sixties. The Marine Corps RF-4B
(originally F4H-1P) was preceded by the Air
Force RF-4C (originally RF-110A), both logical
choices for a new generation of machines in the
picture-taking and intelligence-gathering role.

Outwardly not easy to distinguish from the
fighter model, the RF-4C was unarmed except for
a capability to carry a centreline nuclear weapon.
It was more expensive because of its sophisticated
reconnaissance sensors and communications
systems. The F-4C fighter's APQ-72 radar was
replaced by a small APQ-99 set for mapping,
terrain-following and collision avoidance, with the
rest of the re-shaped nose filled with forward
oblique, lateral and panoramic cameras. In the
underside was installed a large SLAR (sideways-
looking airborne radar) giving a high definition
picture strip along the flight path. Further back

*Mystery picture. History has left no record of why—or
how—the first production RF-4C Phantom (63-7740)
carried twelve 820-lb (370 kg) M-117 GP bombs in
November 1965. This RF-4C-17-MC was not equipped or
wired for ordnance. Says McDonnell's Robert S Blake,
'The hard points were on the wing but we couldn't drop the
bombs in an attack mode. Probably, we were asked if it was
possible for the RF's to carry bombs.' An Air Force officer
recalls that the RF-4C may have been rigged to carry and
eject stores as part of a project called Seek Eagle, an
Edwards AFB, California project to test wiring and stores
separation
(MDC)*

was placed an IR (infrared, or heat) linescan
system giving a clear, thermal-image film picture
of the same area. Masses of special
communications and electronics were installed
from nose to tail and would be updated over the
years.

The first of two YRF-4C prototypes (62-12200)
was resplendent in gull gray and white paint with
the buzz number FJ-200 and a temporary 'candy
stripe' pitot boom, instrumented for precise yaw,
roll and pitch readings. (Until discarded in 1965,
buzz numbers, literally intended to help spectators
identify low-buzzing pilots, were carried on the
side of the fuselage and on the underside of the
fuselage between the engines on F-4C and RF-4C
aircraft). The YRF-4C of August 1963 was
followed by the first actual RF-4C in May 1964.
RF-4Cs would be rushed into service quickly: RF-
4C pilot training began at Shaw AFB, South
Carolina with the 363 Reconnaissance Wing's 4415

Combat Crew Training Squadron on 19 January 1965. On 12 May 1965, the first Phantoms in Europe were two RF-4Cs (64-1019, 64-1025) which arrived at RAF Alconbury where the 10 TRW would have three squadrons totalling 36 aircraft operational by 19 December 1965. Almost as quickly, the reconnaissance machine was, by 15 October 1965, flying out of Saigon's Tan Son Nhut Airport with the 11 TRS.

Gray-white F-4C fighters followed the reconnaissance model to Europe. F-4Cs arrived with the 81 TFW at RAF Bentwaters, England on 2 March 1966. For a decade to come, the Phantom would bulwark the American commitment to NATO and would eventually serve at Lakenheath, Zweibrucken, Soesterburg, Bitburg, Spangdahlem, Ramstein.

Rolling Thunder

Six months after the Gulf of Tonkin air strikes, on 13 February 1965, President Lyndon B Johnson authorized a sustained offensive campaign against North Vietnam code-named Rolling Thunder. By this time, Hanoi's air force had 70 MiG-15 and MiG-17 fighters and was soon to receive MiG-21s.

The MiG-17, a completely redesigned development of the Korean War MiG-15, dated to about 1955 and was 'old' but it was also highly manoeuvrable and remained an ideal machine in a close-in dogfight, especially against American adversaries who were required to be within visual range before firing. Powered by a 7,500-lb (3,400 kg) thrust Klimov VK-1 turbojet, the MiG-17 was armed with three 23-mm NR-23 or one 37 mm NR-37 and two NR-23 cannon and could also carry Atoll air-to-air missiles. Guns, an asset not possessed by the Phantom, would mean much in the battle ahead.

The MiG-21F was a more advanced, delta-winged fighter much closer to the state of the art. Although somewhat crude by American standards, it was also lightweight and highly manoeuvrable. Powered by a Tumansky R-11 turbojet delivering 12,676 lb (5,750 kg) thrust with afterburning, the MiG-21F could carry two AA-2 Atoll missiles and a single 30 mm NR-30 cannon. Controllable up to high angles of attack and low airspeeds, the MiG-21, too, would possess an advantage by virtue of packing a gun.

The Phantom could carry the AIM-4D Falcon air-to-air missile under inboard pylons, but rarely did. The Falcon had been designed for the air intercept role and would have been effective against enemy bombers, but it was not the weapon to take 'downtown'—to Hanoi. In 1965, the principal punch of the Phantom was the AIM-7 Sparrow radar-guided air-to-air missile. The Sparrow was 12 ft (3.65 m) long, had a launch weight of 400 lb (200 kg), and carried a 60-lb (30 kg) high explosive warhead to an accurace range of up to fourteen miles (22 km). It was the most effective possible weapon when the other guy didn't know it was coming and when the attacking Phantom crew faced no risk of losing its radar 'lock-on.'

Also arming the Phantom was the AIM-9 Sidewinder, the AIM-9E model being in use in 1965. This was an infrared homing (heat-seeking) air-to-air missile 9 ft (287 cm) long, with a launch weight of 160 lb (86 kg), which carried a 10-lb (4.5 kg) high explosive warhead over a two-mile (3.7 km) range. The Phantom routinely carried up to four each, Sidewinders and Sparrows.

As it turned out, the first MiG kills of the war would go to the Navy—two MiG-17s shot down by carrier-based Phantoms of the 'Freelancers' of squadron VF-21 on 17 June 1965. Cdr Louis C Page, Jr and Lt John C Smith, Jr, flying an F-4B Phantom (151488), coded NE-101, callsign SUNDOWN 101, got their MiG-17 with an AIM-7 Sparrow. The North Vietnamese also suffered the off-beat indignity of having a MiG-17 shot down by a propeller-driven Douglas A-1H Skyraider on 20 June 1965. Then it was the Air Force's turn.

On 10 July 1965, four F-4Cs from the 45 TFS 15 TFW stationed at Ubon were escorting Republic F-105 Thunderchief strike aircraft when they tried a new tactic—delaying their arrival over target until the F-105s were about to drop their ordnance, the point at which North Vietnamese pilots considered the 'Thuds' most vulnerable and, in turn, exposed themselves.

To conserve fuel, the lead element of two F-4Cs chose not to use afterburners and the trailing element flew an 'S' pattern behind the leaders. This kept the elements close—too close to use radar-guided Sparrows—as they sighted and turned behind a hostile flight of MiG-17s. The Americans overshot, rolled to the right into a 30-degree dive, then turned into the MiGs.

A close-in dogfight ensued. The Americans wished they had guns but used Sidewinders. The two crews, consisting of Capt Kenneth E Holcombe and Arthur C Clark, and Capts Thomas S Roberts and Ronald C Anderson, each accounted for a MiG-17. In keeping with the Air Force practice quickly adopted, each of the two men aboard a Phantom was given full credit for a kill. The battle put them into a 'tight' fuel situation which would imperil Phantom crews throughout the war and they landed at Udorn, which was closer than Ubon, with 1,800 lb (820 kg) of fuel left in one F-4C and only 275 lb (120 kg) in the other, not even enough for a 'go-around.' (The 'low fuel' warning light on the F-4C lights up at 2,000 lb (907 kg) fuel remaining with a gauging accuracy of plus/minus 200 lb (90 kg)). Hearing about the first Air Force kills while on

leave at the Princess Hotel in Bangkok, Lt
Kenneth W Cordier joined other 45 TFS pilots to
celebrate jubilantly.

The F-4C, flown by two full-fledged pilots with
full dual controls, now began to proliferate. From
this point onward, the Phantom story would
become too complex for each individual squadron
to receive mention. Though the bulk of air-to-
ground operations in Rolling Thunder were being
borne at this time by the F-105, with top cover
from Phantoms, the Phantom would eventually
take on both the fighter and strike roles.

By December 1965, the 8th Tactical Fighter
Wing, the 'Wolfpack,' was operating out of Ubon.
Soon thereafter, the 35 TFW went to Da Nang
and the 366 TFW, the 'Gunfighters,' to Phan
Rang. The Air Force decided to camouflage its
Phantoms—'the first attempts were crude,' says
Cordier, 'they added 300 lb (130 kg) of weight to
the aircraft and if your flight leader *wasn't*
camouflaged, he had to give you five per cent
power so you could stay with him'—and soon
afterward came two-letter tailcodes. The North
Vietnamese decided to confront them with MiG-

INSET
Although some reports indicate that a Chinese MiG was downed on an earlier date, the first North Vietnamese MiG shot down in the war, and the first of the Rolling Thunder campaign, fell to Cdr Louis C Page, Jr and Lt John C Smith, Jr. The men, of the 'Freelancers' of squadron VF-21, used an AIM-7 Sparrow to shoot down a MiG-17 on 17 June 1965 while flying an F-4B Phantom (151488), coded NE-101, callsign SUNDOWN 101. Their Phantom later became a casualty of North Vietnamese AAA fire while flying with a different squadron on 17 November 1967
(US Navy)

F-4C Phantoms bombing from altitude over North Vietnam, the aiming performed by the Douglas EB-66 Destroyer leading this formation. In 1965, Phantoms in Vietnam were still gull gray and, like these, wore Tactical Air Command (TAC) badges even though assigned to Pacific Air Forces (PACAF). Closest aircraft in picture, F-4C-20-MC 63-7640, is listed as being lost in Vietnam on 13 September 1968
(US Air Force)

21s. A tangle with the new, Soviet-built fighter was practically thrown into the faces of Maj Paul J Gilmore and 1st Lt William T Smith aboard an F-4C Phantom (64-752) of the 480 TFS 35 TFW on a mission from Da Nang on 26 April 1966. Gilmore hit his adversary with a Sidewinder and the crew became the first Americans to down a MiG-21.

Rolling Thunder was the first of two major American campaigns against North Vietnam. It would run from 13 February 1965 until 31 October 1968 when President Johnson imposed a total bombing halt in the North. While it brought devastation closer and closer to Hanoi, raising the cost to the enemy of supporting and supplying the insurgency in the South, critics held that it didn't always roll and wasn't consistently thunderous.

There were ever-changing rules about which targets could be attacked and which could not. For a period, decisions as routine as the ordnance carried on a mission were made as far from Saigon

F-4C Phantom (63-7544) of the legendary 8th Tactical Fighter Wing's 'Wolfpack,' on a combat mission in Vietnam, November 1966 (US Air Force)

as the White House. For most of the three and a half years of the campaign, it was permissible to engage the enemy's growing MiG force in the air but MiGs could not be attacked on the ground. Even in the air, North Vietnamese fighter commanders often seemed to outthink and outfight their American counterparts.

The enemy had the advantage of fighting over his home ground, in poor weather which favoured the defender at least during the April-to-October monsoon season. He was backed by a staggering array of radar-directed anti-aircraft artillery (AAA, or 'Triple A') and surface-to-air missile (SAM)

weaponry—the latter in the form of the Soviet-supplied SA-2 Guideline missile. The Americans needed to travel far to engage, using midair refuelling routinely on combat missions for the first time in history. They needed to bring enormous amounts of fuel and ordnance with them, and had to dodge flak and SAMs while striking targets and tangling with MiGs. They were also set back by the bomb shortage in late 1966: The F-4C, which by then was supplanting the F-105 in the air-to-ground role, could routinely carry six 750-lb (340 kg) bombs on a long mission but sometimes went against a target with two 250-pounders (114 kg).

The Air Force F-4C was active in the 'in country war' in South Vietnam as well as the 'out country war' against targets in the North.

In the south, tactics were devised to make best use of ground-to-air communications and of Forward Air Controllers (FACs) flying Cessna O-1 Bird Dogs and later Cessna O-2 Skymasters to identify, pinpoint, and mark targets such as Viet Cong troop concentrations. Phantom crews exposed themselves to small-arms, 37-mm cannon fire and (toward the end of the war) shoulder-mounted SAMs. Men returned from missions sometimes not knowing what, if anything, had been hit by their ordnance. They also returned with gaping shell holes in wings, tail, even fuselage—testimony to the Phantom's ruggedness. In time, the Phantom replaced the North American F-100D Super Sabre (surprisingly, the only fighter type to fly more *hours* than the Phantom in the Vietnam war) and supplanted the Cessna A-37 and other types to take on the main burden of the 'in country war.' The struggle in the south was bitter and difficult, and the risk of capture was especially frightening because of the primitive conditions under which the Viet Cong guerillas moved about. But no MiGs ever challenged US command of the south's skies and, inevitably, it was the fight in the north to which every fighter pilot's instincts turned.

On paper, to make it unnecessary to use foreign names in routine communications, US officers divided North Vietnam into six regions, known as Route Packages, Route Packs, or RPs. The most fiercely-defended sector of the enemy homeland, Route Package Six (properly written with the roman numeral VI) encompassing the Red River basin, Hanoi and Haiphong, was where the best targets and the most MiGs could be found. Men who flew into this region, and who would later

OVERLEAF
After the adoption of camouflage but before tailcodes came into use, F-4C Phantom (63-7544) and wingmates refuel from KC-135A tanker on a Rolling Thunder mission in 1966
(US Air Force)

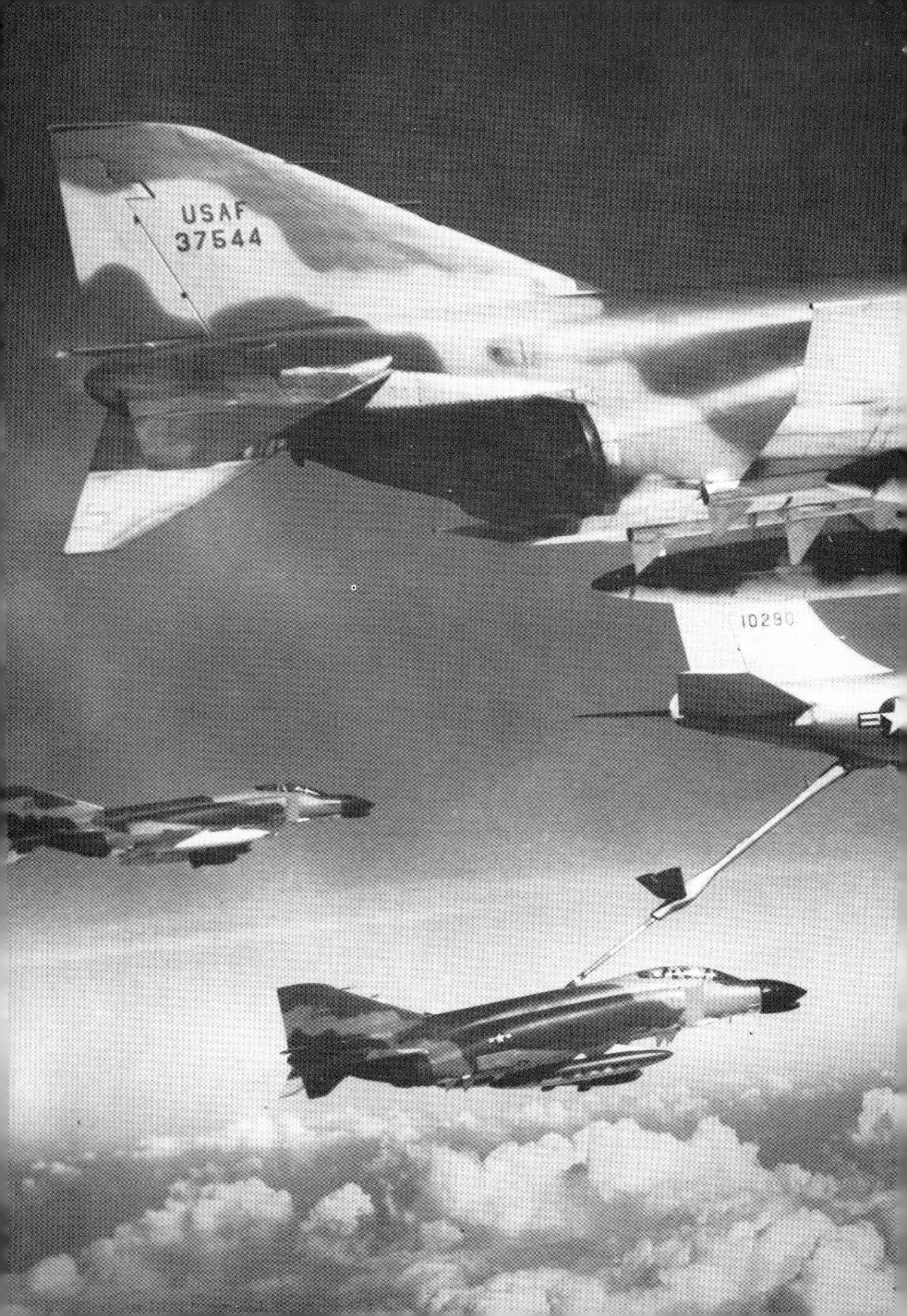
USAF
37544
10290

create a fraternity called the Red River Rats, faced
the prospect of death or capture on any given
day—and being captured, as it turned out, could
mean being a prisoner of war (POW) for up to
eight years. Because of lessons learned in the early
part of the Rolling Thunder period, Phantoms
going against Route Package VI had direct support
by 1966 from an airborne early-warning Lockheed
EC-121 Constellation, called RIVET TOP and,
later, DISCO. A US Navy tracking vessel in the
Gulf of Tonkin, called RED CROWN, also
warned of MiG activity. RED CROWN and
DISCO tracked enemy fighter movements on
radar and warned pilots approaching North
Vietnam when and where they would be
intercepted. It can be assumed that enemy ground
control intercept (GCI) communications were
monitored as well.

The 'out country war' moved in fits and starts.
During the first half of 1966, MiGs engaged
American aircraft on an average of only once a
month. Soon, however, the conflict heated up
again. The threat from AAA, SAMs and MiGs
grew progressively worse, threatening the ability of
strike forces to bring their ordnance to bear on
targets. A feeling was growing that some decisive
step was needed to neutralize the MiG threat.

From that period comes a legend of a bold
North Vietnamese fighter wing commander—the
enemy counterpart of Col Robin Olds of the 8

TFW's Wolfpack at Ubon—who led MiG formations with unusual skill and daring. One published work identifies this man as Col Tomb, another as Comrade Toon, although neither is a name in the Vietnamese language. In any event, the Soviet-trained North Vietnamese pilots were rarely as aggressive as the legend would suggest. Their standard tactic was to loiter at a safe distance (unlike the Americans, having no need to conserve fuel) and to move into battle only with a clear opportunity to attack American aircraft, usually F-105s too burdened with ordnance to fight back. North Vietnamese literature would later credit one very young-looking lieutenant with 13 air-to-air kills. But Hanoi has never confirmed Col Tomb's role or demonstrated that it genuinely

LEFT
*F-4J Phantom (155550) of VMFA-334, a short-lived Marine Corps Phantom squadron, at MCAS Iwakuni, Japan in about 1967
(Tsunehiro Kouda)*

*At a Vietnamese airbase guarded by Hawk surface-to-air missiles (left), Marine Corps' F-4B Phantom (150446) of the 'Gray Ghosts' of VMFA-531 lands after a strike mission. F-100 Super Sabres are parked in revetments behind the runway
(MDC)*

produced fighter aces. During Rolling Thunder, Col Olds—already credited with 24½ victories in P-38s and P-51s during World War II—would score four of the five kills needed for ace status.

One reason for the low air-to-air activity in 1966 was the weather. 'The weather was usually lousy,' says Col Kenneth W Cordier. The effectiveness of SAMs forced American aircraft down to altitudes of around 5,000 ft (1,525 m), too low for the missiles to be effective and too high for risk from light ground weapons. Bomb strikes were frequently carried out in heavy cloud cover and rain. On some missions, the point of bomb release was determined by Douglas EB-66 electronic warfare aircraft which accompanied the fighter-bombers to their targets.

Black Friday

The increasing potency of Hanoi's defenses was to take its toll, as Cordier found out. It all came to a head on 2 December 1966—'Black Friday,' in Cordier's parlance.

On that date, US aircraft conducted strikes against petroleum facilities in Route Package VI. F-105s of the 388 TFW from Korat and F-4Cs of the 366 TFW, which had now moved from Phan Rang to Da Nang, were tasked to strike the Phuc Yen oil storage facilities. F-4Cs from Cordier's 12 TFW out of Ubon were charged with flying cover to guard against MiGs. The strikes had a devastating, if temporary, impact on the North Vietnamese ability to wage war, but when the smoke had cleared *eight* American aircraft and crews were lost. The breakdown:

Early morning: An F-4C Phantom (64-663) of the 389 TFS 366 TFW, callsign CHICAGO 1, was hit by a SAM in the tail. With the aircraft on fire, both crew members ejected and were taken prisoner. The aircraft commander, Maj Burns, would survive captivity and be released with most POWs seven years later. His back-seater, Lt Ducat, would die in captivity.

Early morning: Another F-4C Phantom (64-753) of the 480 TFS 366 TFW was on MiG combat air patrol (MiGCAP) guarding the attackers of the Phuc Yen storage facilities. The aircraft was hit by a SAM and the crew ejected. Both crew members, Capt Flesher and Lt Berger were captured and would be held by the North Vietnamese until their release in March 1973.

Late morning: An F-105D striking Phuc Yen was hit by another of the ubiquitous SAMs and crashed, killing the pilot. Shortly thereafter, an RF-4C reconnaissance Phantom (65-829) was lost on a photo-taking mission. The role of the 'recce' Phantom had grown increasingly important as the Rolling Thunder commitment deepened, and unarmed recce crews routinely accepted terrible risk as part of their official mandate to '*protect the force'* and *'get the pictures.'* This RF-4C was from the 432 Tactical Reconnaissance Wing which, later in the war, would operate fighters as well, adding to its official mission a third chore described on a sign at Udorn: *'. . . and kill MiGs.'* The crew of 65-829 ejected but apparently only the back-seater survived to be released as as POW seven years later.

Later in the day: A Navy F-4B Phantom (151014) from the 'Black Knights' of VF-154 aboard *Coral Sea* (CVA-43) and two A-4C Skyhawks in action around Kep airfield were shot down, again apparently by SAM missiles which were being unleashed in furious barrages.

And finally, late in the day: Another F-4C Phantom (63-7608) of the 559 TFS 12 TFW was in the battle zone escorting an EB-66 mission against the troublesome SAM sites which had already wreaked so much havoc. While orbiting at 21.30°N, 150.00°W, this Phantom was struck by yet another SAM which caused a fire and injured the pilot. The crew ejected. Lt Lane, the back-seater, would survive his seven year stint as a POW. Now on his second tour of combat duty in Southeast Asia, the front-seat aircraft commander who ejected with Lane was Col Kenneth W Cordier—at the time a captain and the man who had expressed so much enthusiasm for the

Phantom when it first arrived at MacDill four years earlier. Cordier was injured and severely burned when his ejection seat blew him into space and his parachute began to unfurl.

As Air Force officer Don Jay says, 'It was a bad day for us.' Bad enough that SAMs and Triple-A were disrupting bomb strikes, the missions in the final weeks of 1966 also brought about a newly aggressive and darkly dangerous MiG threat. Col Tomb had fashioned a world-class fighting force. *Something had to be done . . .*

Enter Robin Olds. Enter Chappie James.

Olds had been an all-American tackle at West Point before racking up 24½ kills in Europe in World War II. He'd been so angry about missing out on the Korean War he could barely speak of it. A well-loved, shrewd, aggressive fighter wing commander, perfect to be pitted against Col Tomb, Robin Olds was the kind of man who might have uttered the words actually spoken as long ago as the First World War by Baron

F-4B Phantom (152227) of the 'Aardvarks' of VF-114 preparing for catapult shot from USS Kitty Hawk *(CVA-63) about 1966*

Manfred von Richthofen: '*The fighter pilots have to rove in the area allotted to them . . . and when they spot an enemy they attack and shoot him down. Anything else is rubbish . . .*'

Col Daniel 'Chappie' James, deputy commander of the Wolfpack, at six feet two was so big he didn't climb into an F-4C; it was said that you wedged him into it with a shoehorn. In 1943, fresh from college, eager to fly and fight, he was assigned to an all-black unit—standard practice before President Truman integrated the armed forces in 1951. James fought for civil rights before it was easy or fashionable, fought his country's enemies from fighter cockpits, and would wear the four stars of a full general before his untimely death in 1978. With Olds, with other men in Phantoms, Chappie James now schemed to take out North Vietnam's fighter force.

Col Robin Olds, WW II fighter ace and commander of 8th Tactical Fighter Wing's 'Wolfpack' at about the time of Operation Bolo, when Old's Phantom crews shot down seven MiGs in one day with no losses (Frank MacSorley)

BELOW
Col Daniel 'Chappie' James, key figure in Operation Bolo, flew everything from P-51 Mustangs to F-4C Phantoms. James never got a MiG, nor did the Phantom (63-7499) shown with a full ordnance load in this photo, but James did reach four-star rank as a general. He was one of the outstanding men in Robin Olds' 8th Tactical Fighter Wing, the 'Wolfpack' (US Air Force)

Believed to be an actual shot of a take-off for Operation Bolo, photo shows a much-weathered F-4C Phantom with full load of Sparrow and Sidewinder air-to-air missiles taking off (US Air Force)

Operation Bolo

It has become fashionable to write that the Bolo mission was plotted by top brass in Washington, at PACAF headquarters in Hawaii, or in Saigon. It was not. Credit for the Bolo scheme belongs to a very junior captain, John B Stone, who—with other young men in Phantoms—persuaded James and Olds. Robin Olds then went to the brass and got the okay for the assault on Col Tomb.

The plan was simple. It would probably work only once. Still proscribed from attacking MiGs on the ground, F-4C Phantom crews would have to lure the enemy aloft, bait him into exposing himself, and strike. The key was the enemy's inability to distinguish one aircraft type from another using his radar. For the 2 January 1967 mission, F-4Cs would follow a flight profile 'acting' like ordnance-laden F-105Ds. Col Tomb's men, mistakenly believing the strike force was an easy target, would be tricked into engaging without the benefit of surprise, speed or altitude.

The configuration of the F-4C for the Bolo mission reveals both the development and the flexibility of McDonnell's fighter. By this point, late-production F-4Cs had come off the line without the 'chin pod' IR probe built on earlier F-4Cs, so their radomes—precisely identical to those of the F-4D to follow—had a clean, bullet-like shape. Camouflage was now standard for the F-4C and two-letter tail-codes were beginning to appear. At this juncture, the 8 TFW carried codes assigned by *squadron* (FO for the 435 TFS, FY for the 555 TFS, and so on) while the 366 TFW—which flew from Da Nang in support of Bolo—would soon acquire individual codes for each *aircraft* (AK for 64-776, AT for 64-820). The latter system would last only briefly, represented by the aircraft flown by Lt Col Robert F Titus and 1/Lt Milan Zimer when they came as close as anyone would to Olds' record by downing three MiGs in 1967. The system based upon squadron assignment would last until mid-1972 when the Air Force finally assigned tailcodes to *wing* rather than squadron units.

For Bolo, Olds' F-4C Phantoms of the 8 TFW's Wolfpack were configured asymmetrically with a fuel tank under one wing and an electronic countermeasures (ECM) pod under the other, a centreline fuel tank, four Sidewinders, and four Sparrows. Olds commanded the full strike force of fourteen flights of F-4Cs, six flights of 'Iron Hand' F-105s configured for SAM suppression, and four flights of Lockheed F-104C Starfighters, the last-named being an aircraft type which served only

briefly in the battle zone. Radio callsigns for the Bolo mission were a word-play on the colonel's name and names of automobiles—OLDS, FORD, and RAMBLER flights.

Over Phuc Yen, which was a MiG base as well as an oil storage depot, Olds' wingman radioed a MiG-21 warning just as another flight leader did the same. Other MiG-21s were coming up from a thin layer of low cloud. Olds began a sharp left turn in his F-4C (63-7680, coded FP) to throw off the onrushing MiG-21 while keeping flight discipline intact. Immediately, he spotted another aircraft in the eleven o'clock position in a left turn ahead of him. This was an all-silver MiG-21. He closed in.

Olds instructed his back-seater, 1/Lt Charles C Clifton, to prepare for an attack with AIM-7, radar-guided Sparrow missiles. But they were closing so rapidly that their decision time had virtually run out. Here was the classic situation

F-4C Phantom 64-848, coded FP, of the 497th Tactical Fighter Squadron, 8th Tactical Fighter Wing, 'Wolfpack', armed with Sparrow and Sidewinder AAMs during Rolling Thunder operations against North Vietnam (Frank MacSorley)

where a gun would have been a godsend, but no Phantom was armed with guns at this time. Olds fired two Sparrows but lost radar lock-on before they could reach the target.

He shifted to the heat-seeking AIM-9 Sidewinder. A 'growl' in his earphones gave the signal that the heat-seeker had acquired the target. But the MiG was fast receding toward cloud. Olds fired and missed.

While his wingman busily chased the MiG-21 which had triggered the initial warning, Olds spotted another MiG-21 to his left just above the clouds. Olds pulled sharply to the left, turned inside the new adversary, and lifted his nose. He then went into a violent barrel roll to the right which put him and Clifton upside-down in relation to the horizon. Inverted, they closed on the MiG, waiting for deflection and range parameters to be right. In seconds, Olds had snapped out of the roll and, at .95 Mach, was pulling below and behind the left side of the MiG.

A 'growl' again. Olds fired two Sidewinders. The first veered sharply to stay with the target, caught the MiG, and set off a blinding, red-yellow explosion. The MiG literally fell apart, pieces of one wing narrowly missing a collision with Olds— a radiant sight of brilliant colour and motion, fire and smoke. Its pilot never got out. Olds and Clifton had a kill.

Chappie James in OLDS 4 was not to get a MiG kill, though he tangled with them at close quarters that day. James was aware that plans were afoot to add a gun to the Phantom's armament— first, with an external pod for the F-4C and F-4D, later with an internally-mounted weapon on the F-4E. He favoured this. After all, the MiGs were armed with 23-mm and 37-mm cannons, as well as an Atoll missile which seemed a carbon copy of the Sidewinder. Meanwhile, James was close to MiGs on several occasions but did not score a confirmed kill.

When the dust had cleared, *seven* MiG-21s had fallen in battle. No American aircraft had been lost and the North Vietnamese air force had been dealt a crippling blow. The Air Force squadrons involved in the kills were the 433 TFS and 555 TFS, the latter the famous 'Triple Nickel' unit which by now had become part of Olds' 8 TFW. Less publicized, of course, was the support provided by the Phantom-equipped 366 TFW and the many other units with other types of aircraft, including the all-important KC-135 tankers.

Chappie James would later say that the tanker crews were the ones who ought to have medals. Just as a fighter crew revelled in claiming a kill when a MiG fell in its sights, a tanker crew would celebrate a 'save' when it enabled a fuel-starved Phantom to 'gas up' and return safely to base. Often, a tanker would provide small amounts of fuel to each of several fighters in turn, then return

to 'top off' the first so that an entire flight could be saved from a watery grave in the Gulf of Tonkin. On one occasion, a battle-damaged Phantom was leaking fuel more rapidly than the KC-135 could replenish it: The tanker hooked on and towed the Phantom back to Da Nang.

OPPOSITE PAGE
A Rolling Thunder MiG killer and a survivor, F-4C Phantom 64-660 was serving with the 136th Fighter Interceptor Squadron, New York Air National Guard, when this photo was taken at Niagara Falls in 1983. During the 1965–67 campaigns over North Vietnam, this F-4C accounted for three MiG-17s while flown by three different American crews, the MiG kills being represented by the three red stars painted on the engine intake variable splitter ramp
(D F Brown)

The great fighter wing commander of an era, Col Robin Olds, at left, with Capt John B Stone, the junior officer credited with devising Operation Bolo. On 2 January 1967, these two front-seat pilots were among the men from the 8th Tactical Fighter Wing's Wolfpack which shot down seven MiGs in a single day. F-4C Phantom (63-7499) in background is typical of the aircraft they flew when they prevailed over North Vietnam's Colonel Tomb (US Air Force)

Two days after Operation Bolo, two more MiGs were shot down by Phantom crews and, later in 1967, the ban on striking enemy airfields was briefly lifted.

Gun Pod

Fighting in both South and North Vietnam increased steadily throughout 1967. In the skies over the North, MiG pilots became more aggressive. Some reports have indicated that Russian and North Korean pilots were helping the North Vietnamese. With or without such help, Hanoi had now had time to develop a trained and dedicated fighter force and had a cadre of pilots who were both skilled and tenacious.

The centreline-mounted, external gun pod had been in use for air-to-ground work. One Phantom officer recalls, 'My favourite load was two tanks, two cans of napalm, and the cannon. I killed about 200 NVA one day on a low-level strafing run.' For *air-to-air* use against Col Tomb's growing MiG force, the SUU-16/A gun pod using a ram air turbine to electrically fire its 20-mm M61 cannon began to arrive in South Vietnam in May 1967 and the first examples went to the 366 TFW at Da Nang, the aptly named 'Gunfighters.' The SUU-16/A can also be operated hydraulically. (A later generation of Phantom pilots, including today's, would carry the SUU-23 gun pod with a gas-operated GAU-4 20-mm cannon). Da Nang's men began fighting with guns on 14 May. From that

TOP LEFT
F-4D Phantom 66-8775, coded CO (the only aircraft ever to be so coded), nickname 'The Saint', the personal mount of the commander of the 366th Tactical Fighter Wing at Da Nang, the 'Gunfighters', during Rolling Thunder (T H Brewer)

BOTTOM LEFT
Col Robin Old's F-4C Phantom 64-829, coded FG, 8th Tactical Fighter Wing, with two MiG kills on the splitter plate. Olds eventually shot down four MiGs (Frank MacSorley)

BELOW
One of twelve datalink F-4G Phantoms (150642), which later reverted to F-4B standard, in briefly-used experimental green camouflage, operating from USS Kitty Hawk (CVA-63) during Rolling Thunder combat operations

OVERLEAF
Toting an ECM pod in its forward right Sparrow bay, F-4D Phantom (66-8761) of the 8th Tactical Fighter Wing's 'Wolfpack' taxies in from Southeast Asia mission

INSET
All black, no markings, only shark teeth—but no cloak-and-dagger story here. Marine Corps F-4B Phantom being refinished in primer paint at Da Nang in February 1969 where a neighbouring Air Force unit seems to have 'zapped' the machine with a sharkmouth
(MDC)

Foam-covered, less damaged than it looks, F-4C Phantom (64-666) of the 12th Tactical Fighter Wing was brought to a belly landing by Maj Robert D Russ and 1/Lt Douglas M Melson at Cam Ranh Bay following a June 1968 combat mission
(US Air Force)

day on, no MiG pilot could ever count on confronting an Air Force Phantom that couldn't bring a gun to bear in a point-blank gunfight. The Navy, which tested gun pods mounted under the *wings* rather than the centreline, never adopted a gun pod for operational use.

Another new arrival in Southeast Asia in the spring of 1967 was the F-4D Phantom II. The F-4D differed from the F-4C in having an APQ-109 radar fire-control system and the ASN-63 inertial navigation system, both changes reflecting a conscious decision to be no longer bound by the design characteristics of the Navy's Phantom. Of all the misconceptions about the Phantom ever to appear in print, the most widespread is that the F-4D had a larger radome than the F-4C. It did not. Before the end of the F-4C production run, the unnecessary 'chin pod' IR probe had been deleted. The F-4C and F-4D had identical radomes.

The F-4D was capable of delivering the new, laser-guided 'smart' bombs, more properly known as Precision-Guided Munitions (PGM), but these would not arrive in theater in time to make a mark on the Rolling Thunder campaign. The F-4D *would* make its mark, however: The new model Phantom scored its first kill on 24 October 1967 when Maj William L Kirk and 1/Lt Theodore R Bongartz shot down a MiG-21. Three days later, three MiG-17s fell to three F-4D crews.

1968 saw heightened tensions in Korea. For a time, it appeared that Phantoms might be fighting in two wars in Asia thousands of miles apart. The seriousness of the Korean situation was illustrated

A survivor of Rolling Thunder, F-4C Phantom 63-7704 shot down a MiG-17 on 14 May 1967, while flown by Capt James T Craig, Jr and 1/Lt James T Talley of the 480th Tactical Fighter Squadron. The aircraft is seen here in October 1982 with the 'Coonass Militia' of the 159th Tactical Fighter Group, Louisiana Air National Guard, at its home station, NAS New Orleans, Louisiana (Don Spering)

LEFT
Members of the 497th Tactical Fighter Squadron, 8th Tactical Fighter Wing, the 'Wolfpack' at a ceremony marking 1,000 combat missions over North Vietnam in Phantoms during the Rolling Thunder campaign

when North Korean MiGs shot down a US Navy EC-121K Constellation, killing all 31 men aboard. No actual Phantom combat occurred in Korea, and the level of tension was soon lowered—but the Phantom would remain on guard on that peninsula until the present day.

In Vietnam, the final Air Force kills of the Rolling Thunder campaign—and the last kills for more than four years—came on 14 February 1968 when two F-4Ds from the 8 TFW's Wolfpack tangled with MiG-17s over the North. Col David O Williams, Jr and 1/Lt James P Feighny, Jr of the wing's 435 TFS piloted an F-4D (tail-code FO) to bag a MiG-17. Maj Rex D Howerton and 1/Lt Ted L Voight II of the 'Triple Nickel' (tail-code FY) claimed the other MiG-17 downed that

day—the last enemy fighter until the Linebacker campaigns of 1972.

For brief periods in 1967, enemy airfields were finally allowed as targets. In May, just as the EC-121 Constellation early warning aircraft became fully operational, strikes against airfields caught 26 MiGs on the ground. In a three-day effort in October, 20 MiGs were also destroyed on their bases.

On 31 March 1968 came President Lyndon B Johnson's dramatic speech revealing that he would not seek re-election and imposing a limited bombing halt effective April 1st. On October 31st, seeking progress at the negotiating table, Johnson brought about a complete halt in all combat operations over the North.

In air-to-air action, the US had lost 56 aircraft, the North Vietnamese 116. Most of the kills had been scored by Phantoms, including those from Navy carriers at Yankee Station in the Gulf of Tonkin. And if a single message stood out in the minds of Phantom crews—who knew that F-86 Sabres had racked up a twelve to one kill ratio over MiGs in Korea, and who now had friends in prison in Hanoi—the message was that a two to one advantage in air combat wasn't good enough. The coming F-4E model with an internally mounted gun might make a difference if there were a rematch—as it turned out, superior training in a later era would be more important—but if Phantoms were ever to go North again, the score would have to be better. And go North they would, for it seemed preordained that there must lie ahead a second round against Col Tomb in the skies of North Vietnam.

Chapter 4
F-4 Variants
The Many Models of the Machine

Outside the Soviet Union, the Phantom was produced in greater numbers than any fighter since the F-86 Sabre. 5,200 is a nice round figure but even the *exact* number built requires discussion. Two McDonnell airframes for Japan, recorded as 'forward fuselage trial kits only,' are not 'counted' by the company. Six airframes for Iran at the end of the production run were apparently completed but never flown. Counting those two Japanese, which flew as completed aircraft, and the six Iranians which never flew at all, McDonnell built 5,076 Phantoms. Mitsubishi in Nagoya, Japan, the only other builder, manufactured 125. Thus, the best figure for the exact number of Phantoms is 5,201.

There could have been more. A further 39 machines for Iran, which would have raised the McDonnell total to 5,115 and the overall total to 5,240, were cancelled after the Islamic revolution. Near the end of the quarter-century St Louis production run, James S McDonnell, founder and board chairman of the remarkable firm which bears his name, is reported to have discouraged further Phantom purchases by arguing a need to 'clear the line' for next-generation F-15 Eagles. Sanford 'Sandy' McDonnell, his son and chief executive of the aerospace giant, is quoted as saying that the price of a Phantom—around $17 million,—or six times its cost a quarter-century earlier, discouraged him from promoting 'Phantoms forever.' But when the last machine was built, the US Air Force still wanted more and Jordan, Singapore and Taiwan were potential buyers.

Till now, serial numbers have appeared in parentheses for the enthusiast who demands to know which specific airframe participated in a given event. The purist really wants the machine identified by its 'constructor's number' or c/n—the number assigned to an airframe by its builder. A number painted on a tail can change—as when an F-4J is transferred from the US Navy to the British Royal Air Force—but a constructor's number, like herpes, is forever.

Pilots don't care. An officer who languished for seven years in the Hanoi Hilton went onward for ten years thereafter wrongly informed about the specific F-4C he'd been flying the day he was shot down, and even assembled a beautiful desk model of the wrong individual airplane. Pilots aren't always attentive to which particular bird they're driving on a particular day.

To illustrate the headaches caused by constructor's numbers, Lockheed assigned c/n 1001 to its first C-130 Hercules and 3001 to its third. In a gesture of mercy, McDonnell began with the number one for its first Phantom and gave consecutive numbers to all which followed. Because constructor's number, or c/n, is an eyesore as well as a headache, the synonymous McDonnell term, 'McAir ship number' is used here. McAir ship 412 is, simply, the 412th Phantom of all variants. As McDonnell test pilot Irving S Burrows says it, 'It's been a habit to refer to the airplanes in our test stable by McAir cumulative production number, rather than customer serial number.' Adds McDonnell's Robert S 'Beaver' Blake, 'The last Navy produced F-4J was McAir ship 4201, and was number 522 of the F-4J variant, and had US Navy bureau number 158379. Our aircraft accounting gives no clues as to when F-4J number 522 or bureau number 158379 was delivered but our records show that McAir ship 4201 was accepted by the US Navy on 7 January 1972 and we were paid for it.'

Because Phantoms churned out of the factory in several variants at a time, different variants are mixed together by this method of identifying the airframes in the order they were built. Thus, McAir ships 412, 413 and 414 are RF-4C, F-4C and F-4B variants respectively.

All McDonnell-built Phantoms have block numbers written in US Air Force style—that is, F-4B-26-MC is block 26, F-4B-27-MC is block 27, and so on. In the 1960s, the US Navy additionally identified the block number with a small letter following the bureau number—that is, 153029z for block 26, 153030aa for block 27, and so on. The latter system is no longer in use. Running consecutively, block numbers are almost never of interest to pilots, occasionally to mechanics, and often to buffs. They *do* have significance. For example, while the F-4E-35-MC does not, F-4Es from block 36 onwards are equipped to operate AGM-65/HOBOS/Paveway electro-optically guided bombs. Block numbers appear in this text, in US Air Force style, where essential.

Further mental gymnastics are required to grasp changes in the method of giving designations to aircraft variants. Legend holds that Secretary of Defense Robert S MacNamara, in 1961, told congressional watchdogs all about the Navy F4H and afterward explained the Air Force F-110—never realizing (though it was never meant as a deception) that he was talking about the same aircraft type. MacNamara raged about being 'sandbagged'—a Washington bureaucratic term meaning you've been had—and ordered the 1962 change in the method of designating aircraft. Together, the F4H and F-110 became the F-4. This caused much, but not all, of the confusion. Some individual airframes have had as many as three designations—for example, F4H-1, F4H-1F and F-4A—without a single nut or bolt being altered.

The following is a description of actual variants of the Phantom and of proposed variants never built. Because details on early proposals appear here for the first time in any publication, some space is devoted to them. Given normal development and future prospects, it is safe to assume that further variants will follow before the Phantom's long life comes to an end in the next century.

F3H-(C)

Dating to 1953, the first proposal by the McDonnell design team under Herman D Barkey was for a 'Super Demon,' a single-engine machine called the F3H-(C) outwardly almost identical to the F3H-2N Demon then serving with the Fleet. Rough sketches of the F3H-(C) uncovered for the first time in preparing this book show a Demon-like fighter 58 ft 10 in (253 m/17.6 mm) long with a wingspan of 36 ft 4 in (101 m 10.9 mm). It was to have been powered by a single Wright J67-W-1

engine, the American equivalent of the Bristol Olympus. This powerplant never materialized as a realistic choice for American aircraft.

Although only a preliminary design, never fleshed out in engineering studies let alone built, the F3H-(C) is fully and rightly the first version of the Phantom. Several further variants would exist in the minds of Barkey and his men, and on draftsman's paper, before the first metal would be cut.

F3H-(E)

Early design efforts proceeded to the F3H-(E) proposal of 1953 which dispensed with the nose-high configuration of the Demon and stood level on its tricycle gear just as the final Phantom would. Its length reduced to 55 ft 9 in (16.7 m 228 mm) and wingspan only trivially to 36 ft 9 in, (10.9 m 228 mm), the F3H-(E) retained the single J67-W-1 engine. With a conventional fuselage not influenced by the area rule or 'Coke Bottle' technology then being discovered, the F3H-(E) also had very conventional swept wings and tail. A derivative, the F3H-E2, still a single-engine design, would be presented as an alternative when a twin-engine design was proposed to the Navy on 15 June 1954.

F3H-G

Usually described as the initial Phantom proposal, the F3H-G was in reality third in the series of designs which led to a flying F-4 Phantom II. By the time the F3H-G proposal took form on Berkey's drawing boards it was a twin-engine fighter, to be powered by two Wright J65-W-4 Sapphire engines, equipped with APQ-50 radar, and armed with four 20-mm cannons. The F3H-G would have been 56 ft long (17 m) with a wingspan of 38 ft 8 in (11.5 m 203 mm) and a height of 16 ft 5 in (4.8 m 126 mm).

F3H-G/H

It was the F3H-G/H design which McDonnell proposed, unsolicited, to the US Navy on 18 September 1953. By the time the F3H-G/H became a full-scale factory mock-up, ready for inspection by company officials on 18 May 1954, only a little of its Demon influence remained evident. The F3H-G/H retained the dimensions cited above for the F3H-G but, for the first time, the General Electric J79 engine was listed as its 'alternate' powerplant.

AH-1

In October 1954, when a US Navy letter of intent was issued for fabrication of two prototype and

The F3H-G/H full-scale mock-up on display for McDonnell company officials at the St Louis plant on 18 May 1954 retains many of the external features of the Phantom's predecessor in the Fleet, the F3H Demon (MDC)

RIGHT
By the time a full-scale mock-up was ready in December 1955, the new aircraft was known as the F4H-1 and its planned Wright J65 engines had been changed to General Electric J79 powerplants. At this stage, the Phantom design still had 'unbent' wings (MDC)

one static test aircraft, the F3H-G designation was changed to AH-1 to reflect the attack role then envisaged for the Phantom-to-be. On 15 April 1955, a letter from the US Navy's Bureau of Aeronautics (later the Bureau of Naval Weapons) to the Chief of Naval Operations replaced the twin J65 engines with J79s.

F4H-1

On 26 May 1955, three years before Bob Little's first flight, a letter from the Chief of Naval Operations recommended changing the designation to what it would fly with, F4H-1. The change was formally made on 23 June 1955. There would never be XF4H-1 or YF4H-1 experimental or service-test aircraft, although both designations have appeared informally for the two initial

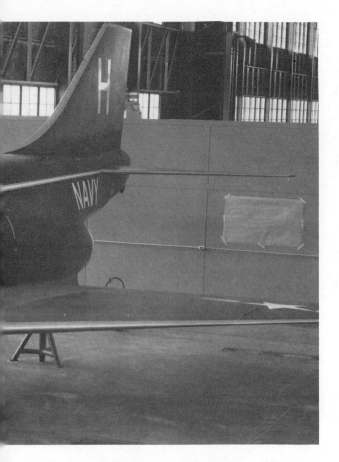

machines. There *would*, however, be *two* different variants to wear the F4H-1 label. From Bob Little's first flight on 27 May 1958 until May 1961, the first 47 Phantoms were designated F4H-1. From May 1961 until the total overhaul of the American system for designating military aircraft on 18 September 1962, the sole use of the F4H-1 designation would belong to the 48th and subsequent production machines. After the latter date, this production F4H-1 would become the F-4B; the proposed F4H-1P reconnaissance craft would fly as the RF-4B; the Air Force F-110A and RF-110A. would become the F-4C and RF-4C respectively.

F4H-1F

In May 1961, the first 47 Phantoms were redesignated F4H-1F. The F suffix indicates a difference in engine type, the 15,000-lb (6,800 kg)

OVERLEAF
The F-4A. Designated F4H-1F at the time this photo was taken, McAir ship 11 (145310) was used in ordnance tests and is shown in 1961 carrying twentry-two 500-lb (227 kg) bombs. This aircraft was accepted by the US navy on 29 August 1959, spent most of its service life in St Louis, and was employed briefly at the Naval Ordnance Test Center (NOTS) at China Lake, California. 145310 now belongs to the Bradley Air Museum in Windsor Locks, Connecticut (MDC)

thrust J79-GE-2 and -2A engines being employed on F4H-1F aircraft during the wait until J79-GE-8A and -8B engines could become available for production aircraft.

F4H-1P

Planning for the Marine Corps reconnaissance version of the Phantom began under the pre-1962 designation system and the F4H-1P designation was applied to the machine which later flew as the RF-4B.

F-4A

Again redesignated, the first 47 machines became the F-4A on 18 September 1962.

Apart from the engine difference cited above, perhaps the most remarkable fact about the 'first 47' is that assigning a single designation to all fails to take into account the major change in basic configuration which took place between the 18th and 19th Phantoms built.

The first 18 F-4As had the top line of the canopy flush with the fuselage, reducing supersonic drag but, also, visibility. They had a different nose shape because of the 24-inch (60 cm) radar antenna mounted up front. Beginning with the number 19 F-4A (146817, used to evaluate the Sparrow missile), all aircraft had the raised canopy and the 32-inch (81 cm) radar dish aerial, the same essential configuration as the future B, C and D models.

Among the first 18, each airframe was really a little different from each of the others. For example, F-4A number 12 (145311), flown by Lt Col Thomas H Miller on his 500-km closed-course speed run, was for practical purposes a single-seater, its nose shape altered by the heavy ballast carried in lieu of radar to offset the absence of a back-seat crewman. F-4A number 13 (145312) ended up with NASA at Edwards AFB, California in 1965 where, piloted by future astronaut Elliott See, it was used to test the effects of weightlessness on a back-seat 'crew' of laboratory frogs.

F-4A number 9 (145308), first flown 21 September 1959 by company pilot Thomas Harris, was involved in a harrowing incident but one which demonstrated the saving graces of the new design. As a McDonnell employee describes it: 'On flight number six, the bleed air system erupted, causing rapid failure of the No 2 fuel cell

The F-4A. Still called an F4H-1 on 15 April 1960 when this shot was taken at St Louis, McAir ship 9 (145308) was used for aerodynamic and equipment tests until being retired from flight status in 1961. This airplane ended its career as a ground trainer for maintenance personnel at NAS Memphis, Tennessee where it was still located as late as 1978
(David Ostrowski)

followed by a massive fuel leak. The airplane was landed without engine power (engines were shut down at 22,000 ft (6,605 m) because of the fuel leak) using only ram air turbine hydraulic and electric power and windmilling engines. To my knowledge, this was the only time in history an F-4 was dead-sticked in an emergency condition. The military services do not allow this and would have required the pilot to eject. Ironically, this happened just a week or two before a scheduled demonstration of deadstick capability at Edwards by company pilot Don McCracken . . .'

Few F-4A aircraft have survived. The oldest is number 3 (143388) belonging to the Marine Corps Air Museum. The final F-4A airframe, number 47 (148275) has for many years been an outdoor display fixture at the US Naval Academy, Annapolis, Maryland.

TF-4A

After their useful life, F-4A Phantoms were burned up at NAS Lakehurst, New Jersey to train firefighters, or stripped apart at NAS Memphis, Tennessee to train mechanics. US Navy records are unclear on whether these non-flying Phantoms received the TF-4A designation. F-4A number 32 (148260), a ground trainer at Memphis as late as 1980, is the only machine confirmed as having held the TF-4A appellation.

F-4B

First flown by Thomas Harris on 25 March 1961 at St Louis in the form of McAir ship 48 (148363), the F-4B—which had been the F4H-1 before 18 September 1962—was the definitive Navy Phantom and the first in combat. Its production J79-GE-8A and -8B engines had been exhaustively tested on F-4A number two (142260) and, as related in chapter two, the production F-4B was pressed into Navy and Marine Corps service very quickly. It was, in its heyday, the most advanced fighter interceptor in the western world.

The F-4B had APQ-72 radar with a 32-inch (81 cm) dish, the Lear AJB-3 bombing system, folding wings and tailhook, and smaller tyres than all subsequent Phantoms. When inboard pylons as well as the four semi-submerged well mountings under the fuselage were used the F-4B was configured for six AIM-7C Sparrow III semi-active radar homing (SARH) air-to-air missiles. More commonly, four Sparrows plus four AIM-

The F-4B. In colourful markings of an earlier time, F-4B Phantom (149461) of fighter squadron VF-32's 'Swordsmen' with lowered tailhook lands on John F Kennedy (CVA-67) *near Guantanamo Bay, Cuba in November 1968. This aircraft later in its career was converted into a QF-4B target drone* (US Navy)

9B Sidewinder infrared (IR) heat-seeking missiles were carried. A probe air-to-air refuelling receptacle was located on the port side above the engine. Bombload of 16,000 lb (7,257 kg) permitted various ordnance loads including up to eighteen 750 lb (340 kg) bombs of four AGM-12C Bullpup B air-to-surface missiles or fifteen packs of 2.75-inch folding fin aircraft rockets (FFAR).

It was the F-4B which carried the brunt of Navy strikes against North Vietnam from carrier decks during the Rolling Thunder campaign, 1965–68. F-4B crews accounted for 14 MiG kills during Rolling Thunder. Though it lacked a gun, the F-4B had manoeuvrability and flexibility for close-in fighting with the MiG-21 and crews had faith in their missiles. One says, 'We found out in 'Nam that against a low altitude MiG that was manoeuvring, the Sparrow needed some improvement . . .'

651 aircraft were built in the F-4B series, including twelve initially completed as F-4G data-link aircraft and two modified on the production line into YRF-4Cs, before the last machine came off the line in December 1966. Surviving F-4Bs have been converted to QF-4B and F-4N standard. Some are on display, the most interesting being McAir ship 56 (148371), which had been used to test an under-fuselage conformal bomb carriage developed by Boeing—never

F-4B Phantom (151002) in colourful markings of the 'Hell's Angels' of Marine Corps reserve squadron VMFA-321 at Andrews AFB, Maryland in 1974 (US Marine Corps, via M J Kasiuba)

adopted, but part of today's thinking for a re-engined 'Super Phantom'—now exhibited at the David W Taylor Naval Ship Research and Development Center at Carderock, Maryland. No F-4Bs remain flying today. The last F-4B in active service was McAir ship 783 (152217) with the 'Hell's Angels' of Marine reserve squadron VMFA-321 at Andrews AFB, Maryland until January 1978.

NF-4B

Two Phantoms employed in test work at the Naval Air Development Center (NADC), Warminster, Pennsylvania in the 1970s underwent structural modifications which warranted assigning the NF-4B designation.

QF-4B

The role of the Phantom as a target drone began late in its career, not surprising since drones are

built to be shot down. The QF-4B, however, was also designed for piloted as well as unpiloted target duties, for example, where radar-intercept techniques are tested without need to actually destory the aircraft simulating an enemy. Distinctive in the bright-red paint scheme used for drones at the Naval Missile Center, Point Mugu, California, the first QF-4B was McAir ship 50 (148365), delivered in 1972 and demonstrated in unmanned flight while 'driven' from a Vought DF-8A Crusader controller aircraft. Reports of a DF-4B controller variant of the Phantom appear to be inaccurate. Numerous QF-4Bs were shot down over New Mexico in the 1970s in tests of the US Army's Patriot surface-to-air missile.

The 44 airframes converted to QF-4B had restrictions placed on their manoeuvrability, being unable to tolerate the full range of manoeuvres authorized for the fighter version.

RF-4B

First flown on 12 March 1965 at St Louis as McAir ship 671 (151975) with Irving S Burrows as pilot, the RF-4B was the Marine Corps' reconnaissance version and belongs chronologically after the Air Force RF-4C. Used only by the Corps, the RF-4B (originally F4H-1P) is equipped with systems similar to its Air Force counterpart

The QF-4B. Drag chute deployed, a QF-4B Phantom target drone (148365) lands at the Naval Missile Center, Point Mugu, California in April 1972. Seen here with a full crew of two men aboard, the QF-4B was designed to be flown with or without men occupying its seats (US navy)

RIGHT
Phantom variant produced in fewest numbers, RF-4B reconnaissance craft (153095) of Marine Composite Reconnaissance Squadron VMCJ-3 comes home, trailing brake parachute, at MCAS El Toro, California in 1973

(page 47). However, it has the internal crew steps found on all fighter versions of the Phantom but *not* on the RF-4C or RF-4E, which require a ladder. The RF-4B has enjoyed remarkable longevity in part due to a 1978 Sensor Update and Refurbishment Effort (SURE) conducted at NARF North Island, which updated the following systems:
    AN/ASN-92(V) Inertial Navigation Set;
    AN/ASW-25B Datalink;
    AN/AAD-5 Infrared Reconnaissance Set
    AN/APD-10 Side-Looking Airborne Radar (SLAR);
    AN3APN-202 Radar Beacon.
46 RF-4Bs were manufactured in two batches from May 1965 to December 1966 and from January to December 1971. The first batch have

standard F-4B wings which accomodate the 30 × 7.7-in (76 cm 195 mm) mainwheel tyres of the F-4B. The second batch have the larger 30 × 11.5-in (76 cm 291 mm) mainwheel tyres and wing wheel well, necessitating a 'bump' in the wing shape, as found on all subsequent Phantom variants including the Navy F-4J.

From 1966 to 1974, the RF-4B community consisted of three Marine composite reconnaissance squadrons (which also operated EA-6A Intruders), VMCJ-1, VMCJ-2 and VMCJ-3 located at MCAS Cherry Point, North Carolina; MCAS El Toro, California, and MCAS Iwakuni, Japan. In September 1974, to centralize management of resources, the EA-6A fleet was positioned with VMAQ-2 at Cherry Point and *all* RF-4B operations were centralized with the new Marine fighter reconnaissance squadron VMFP-3, 'The Eyes of the Corps,' headquartered at El Toro with detachments at other bases. The first flight of a refurbished Project SURE RF-4B took place in the spring of 1978.

OVERLEAF
Caught aloft by photography's unmatched Harry Gann, Marine Corps RF-4B Phantoms (157346, foreground) display the markings of all four squadrons which used them: From left, VMCJ-3, VMCJ-2, VMCJ-1, VMFP-1 (MDC)

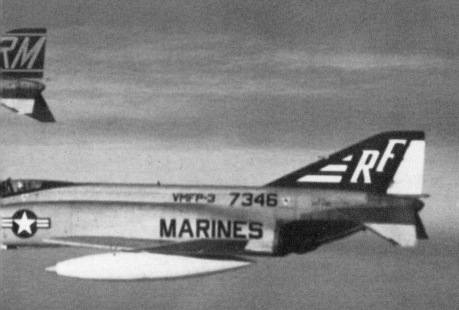

F-110A

The Air Force's pre-September 18 1962 designation for what became the F-4C Phantom was overtaken before any F-4C saw the light of day. Though the aircraft technically wasn't one, for a brief period in 1962 the F-110A appellation was painted distinctively on the nose of McAir ship 122 (149405), one of two Navy F-4Bs painted lavishly in Tactical Air Command markings and used by the Air Force at Edwards AFB.

The F-110A. In January 1962, with snow on the ground in St Louis, US Navy F4H-1 Phantom 149405, the aircraft soon to be designated F-4B, was flying with Tactical Air Command markings and the F-110A appellation painted on its nose. A few months later, in a complete overhaul of the US system for designating military aircraft, what had been planned as the F-110A became the F-4C
(MDC)

TOP
RF-4B Phantom (151981) belonging to VMFP-3, the squadron into which all RF-4B operations were merged in 1974, is shown in operation at NAS Fallon, Nevada on 27 June 1982
(US Marine Corps)

LEFT
An RF-4B from Marine Composite Reconnaissance Squadron One, or VMCJ-1, stationed at MCAS Iwakuni Japan, makes its way over South Korean mountains in 1974. This aircraft (153102) is still in service today with VMFP-3 at MCAS El Toro, California
(US Marine Corps)

F-4C

Its first flight made on 27 May 1963 at St Louis by McAir ship 310 (62-12199), the F-4C reflected the Air Force's preference for the Phantom over other potential candidates, even the controversial TFX, as its prime tactical fighter. For ease of production, the F-4C retained the essential design of the Navy F-4B but to fit service needs some changes were introduced. The nose radome shape, folding wings and tailhook were kept, but larger tyres were used and the rear-seat crewman's position was reconfigured with full dual controls to make him a full-fledged pilot. A less experienced pilot in the back seat had the additional duty of operating the radar, for which 280 hours of radar training was provided. After 'graduating,' this 'guy in back,' or GIB, would move to the front seat to command the aircraft. The technical term for him was pilot systems operator (PSO). This system was changed in 1967–68 when the Air Force decided that, as in the Navy, the Phantom's rear seater should be a non-rated flier, a navigator/weapon systems officer (WSO).

The F-4C was powered by two 17,000-lb (7,700 kg) thrust (with afterburning) J79-GE-15 engines with a self-contained cartridge/pneumatic starter on the wheelcase, not found on the Navy variant. The F-4C had completely revised avionics with APQ-100 radar, Litton type ASN-48 (LN12A/B) inertial navigation system, and a dorsal in-flight refuelling receptacle instead of the Navy's probe.

Though intended for the same armament as the Navy machine—not until the F-4D would the Phantom's air-to-ground potential be fully realized—the F-4C became a more effective dogfighter when configured to carry detachable gun pods, the already-mentioned General Electric SUU-16/A and SUU-23 with M61A1 Vulcan 20-mm cannons.

583 F-4Cs rolled off the line at St Louis before manufacture of this model ceased in February 1966. 40 were subsequently diverted to Spain, the only foreign user, and given the Spanish designation C.12. 36 F-4Cs were temporarily configured for the 'wild weasel' electronic warfare role, but the designation EF-4C was an informal one.

RF-110A

By the time the Air Force's reconnaissance Phantom took to the skies, the new designation system was in use, so no machine ever flew with the name RF-110A.

YRF-4C

First flight by YRF-4C McAir ship 266 (62-12200) piloted by William S Ross (now vice president and general manager for the F-15 program) took place at St Louis on 8 August 1963. Two YRF-4C airframes, modified on the production line from Navy F-4Bs, came before the production RF-4C and subsequently were used in various tests. 62-12200 later served as a YF-4E prototype for the gun-armed F-4E (following). McAir ship 268 (62-12201) is now on outdoor display at Chanute AFB, Illinois.

The F-4C. At the Air Defense Command (ADC) 'William Tell' gunnery meet at Tyndall AFB, Florida in November 1976, F-4C Phantom (63-7436) displays a Bicentennial badge below the rear cockpit, a 'William Tell' arrow and apple on its fuel tank, and the checkerboard markings of the 57th Fighter-Interceptor Squadron stationed at Keflavik AB, Iceland. The 57th FIS, which later converted to the F-4E, was the only Air Defense Command squadron to operate the Phantom

TOP RIGHT
In the arming pits at Spangdahlem, Germany F-4C Phantom (63-7452) of the 52nd Tactical Fighter Wing prepares for a mission. This is one of 36 F-4Cs modified for the Wild Weasel electronic warfare role, informally called EF-4C, and distinguished by a small antenna 'bump' on the fuselage side above the wing root

Pointing its distinctive 'candy stripe' pitot tubes skyward, the first YRF-4C (62-12200) goes aloft on its first flight at St Louis 8 August 1963, with test pilot William S Ross at the controls

RF-4C

With Jack Krings and B A McIntyre aboard, RF-4C McAir ship 412 (66-7740) took to the sky at St Louis, resplendent in gull gray paint with Day-Glo red wingtips and tail, on 18 May 1964. Its principal systems described on page 50, the RF-4C was a fitting replacement for the single-seat McDonnell F-101 Voodoo. It could go in high or low and come back with the pictures. RF-4Cs have undergone changes in systems and nose shapes over the years. The 20 machines in block 40 were equipped with AN/ARN-92 LORAN navigation gear, developed for long-range Vietnam operations and giving the aircraft a distinctive 'towel rack' antenna on the upper rear fuselage.

The RF-4C retains folding wings and tailhook. 18 have been retrofitted with the AN/ALQ-125 Tactical Electronic Reconnaissance (TEREC) equipment package, with 6 more due for retrofit by 1986. Developed by Litton Amecom, this system enables passive precision location of ground-based enemy radar and communications systems in a fully automatic mode. Enemy transmissions are analyzed by computer, correlated with a detailed transmitter bank, and processed into a hostile electronic order of battle (HEOB) display in the rear cockpit. The RF-4C TEREC system is intended to operate in an intense electronic warfare environment with the F-4G Advanced Wild Weasel (following) and the EF-111A Electric Fox to achieve optimum results. To enable it to steer friendly aircraft in attacks on enemy radio/radar sources, RF-4C TEREC aircraft are equipped with Ford AN/AVQ-26 Pave Tack laser designator/fire control systems with limited all-weather capability. This system was first flown aboard an RF-4C test aircraft (69-378) together with a digital datalink pod which would have permitted the HEOB display to be relayed in real time to any interested user on the ground; the datalink pod was not adopted and a real-time capability not acquired.

The back-seat systems operator in the RF-4C has only limited flight controls. His instruments for the reconnaissance function are raised high enough that he has less visibility than his counterpart in a fighter Phantom, especially in TEREC airplanes. He would have to talked down by a wingman to land successfully.

It can be done. On 8 April 1982, WSO 1/Lt Fredric G Wilson was on a night terrain-following mission in an Idaho Air National Guard RF-4C

The RF-4C. A recent picture, its August 1981 date indicated by wraparound camouflage and black tailcodes, photo shows two RF-4C aircraft (66-422 and 66-438) of the 153rd Tactical Reconnaissance Squadron, 186th Tactical Reconnaissance Group, Mississippi Air National Guard, in flight. The KE tailcode comes from the unit's home base at Key Field in Meridian, Mississippi (Don Spering)

when a 20-lb (9 kg) bird shattered the left front windshield and slammed into the pilot, severely injuring him. Wilson took control and made a climbing turn toward Boise, Idaho 115 miles (185 km) east. Though the pilot lowered gear and flaps, he did not communicate with Wilson and Wilson could see that his parachute pack was damaged, ruling out an ejection. Despite almost no visibility because of bird remains on both canopies, Wilson formed on another RF-4C and agreed to try a night formation landing.

The lead RF-4C headed them toward nearby Mountain Home AFB. Wilson's pilot lowered the tailhook, again without communicating. The plan was for an approach-end arrestment for the damaged aircraft, while the lead airplane intended to fly a touch-and-go. In close formation, Lt Wilson flew a 13-mile (20 km) straight-in approach to a successful landing and arrestment. As crash rescue workers arrived to shut down the engines, Wilson safetied the front cockpit ejection seat. He'd saved a pilot and an airplane.

An RF-4C rear-seater accomplished a unique 'first,' one cited here out of respect for history, on 24 May 1982. The American custom of 'mooning'—dropping one's trousers and flashing one's bare posterior toward an onwatcher—was successfully achieved in an RF-4C. A photo taken by a wingman, mercifully ommitted from this text, shows the pilot in helmet and oxygen mask and the unadorned behind of the second crew member. His name and unit are spared the reader.

503 RF-4C Phantoms were built before the final machine was delivered in December 1973. Four RF-4Cs were taken from US Air Force inventory by Spain, the only foreign user, which assigned the designation CR.12.

F-4D

The F-4D represented an effort by the Air Force to alter the Navy design for its own needs, and enhance air-to-ground capability, without major structural rework. It took to the air in the form of McAir ship 1219 (64-929) at St Louis on 9 December 1965, and deliveries began in March 1966.

Outwardly almost identical to previous Phantoms, the F-4D was significantly different in its internal systems. It was equipped with the partly solid-state APQ-109 fire-control radar, although its radome shape was outwardly unchanged. It had a new sight, the ASG-22 lead-computing optical sight, an improved ASG-63 inertial navigation system, and an ASQ-91 weapon release computer making it able to deliver 'smart' bombs or Precision Guided Munitions (PGM).

While it retained four Sparrows in semi-submerged wells under the fuselage as its semi-active radar-homing (SARH) air-to-air armament,

the F-4D was designed with the intent of replacing Sidewinders with four pylon-mounted AIM-4D Falcon missiles as its heat-seeking or infrared (IR) missile arsenal. Tests conducted under Operation Dancing Falcon at Eglin AFB, Florida in late 1965 had indicated the Falcon would be promising for what was then seen as essentially an air-to-ground aircraft. The Falcon had actually been designed as an SARH missile and had been immensely successful, and the same success was foreseen for an IR version which permitted the fighter pilot to break away immediately after launch. Falcons were indeed used by Phantom units through the 1970s but in Vietnam the missile turned out to offer no

The F-4D. The Air Force's 'breakaway' from features of the Navy Phantom, intended to enhance the Phantom's potential in the air-to-ground role and equipped for 'smart' bombs, the F-4D became an effective air-to-air fighter as well and scored numerous MiG kills. In the one-of-a-kind white paint scheme of the Air Force Logistics Center at Hill AFB, Utah, F-4D Phantom 66-7455 is seen in November 1978

The F-4D. Vintage shot of the clean lines of F-4D Phantom 65-620, coded HB, of the 7th Tactical Fighter Squadron, 49th Tactical Fighter Wing, landing at Shaw AFB, South Carolina on 21 September 1968. The 49th Wing is based at Holloman AFB, New Mexico and has since become an operator of the F-15 Eagle (James T Sullivan)

improvement over the Sidewinder which had the same breakaway capability. Pilots found that the Falcon required 'too much finicky setting-up,' or preparation, before launch. Further, because it lacked a proximity fuse the Falcon, unlike the Sidewinder, required a direct hit. After an air battle over North Vietnam in which unsatisfactory Falcon performance may have cost the fifth kill he needed to become a 'Vietnam ace', Col Robin Olds told his maintenance chief that he didn't *care* if the F-4D wasn't designed for Sidewinders, he wanted them installed within 24 hours. This was done. But wiring problems made it possible at first to install only one Sidewinder per inboard pylon rather than the usual two.

Variations and modifications to the F-4D, as to other Phantoms, enabled it to carry an encyclopedic diversity of weapons and ordnance, including gun pods. Eventually, the F-4D inboard pylons were reworked to return to the F-4B/F-4C capability to carry four Sidewinders. The centerline attachment intended for a fuel tank, could be equipped with a multiple ejector rack (MER) for bombs while the inboard pylons could carry a triple ejector rack (TER). F-4D aircraft in block 25 were manufactured with special sensors for Igloo White operations against the Ho Chi Minh trail. The cylindrical Pave Spike laser designator pod for 'smart' bombs occupied one of the fuselage wells for a Sparrow on many F-4Ds, thereby reducing SARH potency by one-fourth. The fatter, drooped Pave Knife laser designator pod could be fitted on an inboard pylon, in lieu of Sidewinders, as could the Westinghouse ALQ-101

The F-4E. With Sparrows, Sidewinders and the 'short' housing for the nose 20-mm cannon, which was later lengthened, two F-4Es of the 43rd Tactical Fighter Squadron at Elmendorf AFB prowl the Alaskan wasteland in about 1973, when incursions by Soviet aircraft were frequent. Aircraft in background (68-425) was lost in an accident 7 January 1974. By 1976, members of this squadron included Capt Roger C Locher who as a WSO evaded North Vietnamese capture for 23 days after ejecting on May 10th, 1972, and Capt Charles B DeBellevue, ranking ace of the Vietnam war (US Air Force)

combination noise and deception jamming pod, the General Electric ALQ-87 barrage noise jammer pod, and other electronic countermeasures (ECM) gear. A modification program code-named Combat Tree in 1968–69 permitted retention of the full missile load while carrying ECM gear, and added a location for an ECM pod to the inboard pylon which by now carried two more advanced AIM-9J Sidewinders on each side.

71 late-production F-4Ds in blocks 32 and 33, like the 20 RF-4Cs already noted, had AN/ARN-92 LORAN navigation gear and dorsal 'towel racks.' Some F-4Ds functioned as electronics warfare aircraft in Vietnam. Two (66-7635 and 66-7647) were tested at Edwards under the informal designation EF-4D from February through April 1976 as unsuccessful candidates for the Advanced Wild Weasel program which produced F-4E conversions to F-4G standard. Two F-4Ds were field-converted in Vietnam under the Pave Arrow program in which a Sidewinder IR heat seeker head was mounted on a fixed pod for use in locating heat sources from ground targets; the

program appears to have been unsuccessful.

Before production ceased in December 1969, 825 F-4Ds were built, 793 for the US Air Force which later turned 36 of these over to South Korea, and 32 for Iran. F-4Ds no longer serve with active US Air Force units but are widely deployed with the Air Force Reserve and Air National Guard in tactical and interceptor roles in continental North America.

YF-4E

McAir ship 266 (62-12200), described earlier as the first YRF-4C, was camouflaged, armed with nose M61A1 cannon, and sent back into the skies as the service-test YF-4E on 7 August 1965 with Joe Dobronski and Ed Rosenmayer on board. Most of the actual firing tests of the 20-mm cannon in this first gun-armed Phantom were performed by George Eaton. Bud Murray flew 266 on its 17 June 1969 first flight in the 'Agile Eagle' program which evaluated fixed leading-edge slats intended to significantly increase lift and thrust-turning performance—leading to the slat installation built on late F-4Es, retrofitted to some early Es, and included in variable (two-position) form on the Navy's F-4S conversion. Though it underwent no further changes in designation in the 737 flights totalling 952.1 air hours of its 15-year career, McAir ship 266 later acquired boron composite and berylium tail surfaces; computer controls in a 'fly-by-wire' test program (first flight 29 April 1972, crew Pete Garrison and Charley Plummer); and became the canard-equipped

The F-4E, with leading-edge slats and lengthened housing for its nose cannon both typical of late airframes in the E-series in flight near St Louis on 30 January 1974. Absence of a TISEO pod on the port wing confirms that 71-1139 is a foreigner—destined for the Imperial Iranian Air Force

Precision Aircraft Control Technology (PACT) or control-configured vehicle testbed (first flight 5 July 1974, pilot Bill Brinks) before retiring to the US Air Force Museum in Dayton, Ohio.

F-4E

Conceived as an improvement over the F-4D with input from Vietnam experience, the F-4E carries the M61A1 Vulcan 20-mm cannon in its nose with provision for 640 rounds, while retaining Sparrow/Sidewinders capability. It also has an additional (seventh) fuel cell in the fuselage which counter-balances the weight of the gun. First flight was made 30 June 1967 at St Louis by McAir ship 2234 (66-284).

The F-4E is equipped with Westinghouse APQ-120 solid-state radar fire control system with a reduced size dish (27.5 in × 24.5 in (67.7 cm 62.1 cm), in eliptical shape). Very late F-4Es near the end of the production run had redesigned, 'ergonometric' (man-efficient) instrument consoles, leading-edge manoeuvre slats, and Northrop's Target Identification System Electro-Optical (TISEO), a TV camera with a 1,200-mm zoom lens in a pod on the leading edge of the port wing.

Alaska's Mount Whitney, highest peak in North America, at right, F-4E Phantom (68-312) of the 43rd Fighter Interceptor Squadron, 21st Composite Wing, heads for 'Jack Frost' winter combat exercise. Capt Charles DeBellevue, top-ranking Vietnam ace, and Capt Roger D Locher, survivor of Vietnam shootdown, were members of the 43 FIS during this period

The principal Air Force and Navy variants of the Phantom are not often seen together. F-4E Phantom 66-330 of the 57th Fighter-Interceptor Squadron flies formation with F-4J Phantom 155781, coded VE-7, of the 'Silver Eagles' of US Marine Corps squadron VMFA-115 near Keflavik AB, Iceland on 7 September 1979. The Marine Corps unit had temporarily taken over the 57th FIS' task of defending NATO's northernmost flank in order to free the Air Force squadron to participate in the semi-annual William Tell gunnery meet at Tyndall AFB, Florida
(Douglas Barbier)

The F-4E can also carry Pave Tack, having tested both the system as adopted and the discarded down-link data pod aboard McAir ship 4238 (71-1070) in a manner to that already described for the RF-4C. F-4Es from 1971 onward have the ARN-101 navigation system. The F-4E can carry most of the items of ordnance already described, including the Pave Spike laser designator and range-finder pod mounted in the port forward Sparrow well. Powered by J79-GE-17 engines which develop 17,900 lb (8,120 kg) static thrust with afterburning, the F-4E is simply *the* version of the Phantom to most users around the world.

831 were manufactured for the US Air Force, which supplied some from inventory to Australia (on loan), Egypt, Israel and Turkey. A further 566 were built for Germany, Greece, Iran, Israel, Japan and Turkey. The total of 1,397 airframes rolled off the St Louis production line between July 1967 and the end of the production run in 1981. 116 have been converted to F-4G Advanced Wild Weasel electronic warfare aircraft and at least one to F-4P. Cannon-armed F-4E fighters are likely to be in service in the next century.

F-4EJ

The designation F-4EJ is used loosely for all Japanese F-4Es, including the 15 built all or in part by McDonnell in St Louis and the 125 manufactured by Mitsubishi in Nagoya, Japan. The last machine in the latter series, with Japan Air Self-Defense Force (JASDF) serial 17-8440, was the final Phantom built and was delivered to the JASDF on May 21st, 1981.

RF-4E

The export reconnaissance version of the Phantom took to the air on 15 September 1970, McAir ship 3861 (69-7448) being the first machine for the first purchaser, West Germany. Though outwardly similar to the RF-4C, the RF-4E was intended for foreign users only and has some of the RF-4C's systems deleted. 150 were built over intermittent periods from September 1970 until the end of the Phantom production run in 1981 for Greece, Iran, Israel, Japan and Turkey.

F-4E(F)

By the late 1960s both McDonnell and the West German Luftwaffe saw benefit in applying the enormous power and load-carrying capability of the Phantom to the single-seat configuration. At the same time, the US Department of Defense held a competition for an export fighter or 'international fighter' (IFX) to be supplied to American allies, with the prospect of lucrative purchase orders from Jordan, Morocco, Korea, Taiwan, South Vietnam, and others. The IFX

needed to be inexpensive and easy to maintain—and the Phantom was neither.

Lockheed proposed the Lancer, a next-generation offspring of the F-104. Vought submitted its V-1000 design. McDonnell proposed a single-seat Phantom, the F-4E(F). The IFX competition was won by Northrop's follow-on to the F-5A Freedom Fighter, which became the F-5E Tiger II, but Bonn remained interested in the F-4E(F). The one-man Phantom variant would have had slats, a new radar, and minimal air-to-air capability as a result of the deletion of its Sparrow SARH missile system. In the event, the German order finally settled on the F-4F (below) and no single-seat Phantom was ever built or flown.

F-4F

'The politest word I can think of is *nonsense*,' says a US Air Force exchange-tour officer who flies the West German F-4F. 'The idea of taking such a capable multi-role fighter and making it a single-seater is nonsense. With such thinking the F-4 becomes a very limited single-role day interceptor.' Apparently, the *Luftwaffe* agreed. The F-4F, outwardly almost identical to the F-4E, retains the second seat and, since its introduction into service, has gradually been upgraded to multi-mission capability.

McAir ship 4330 (72-1111) made the first flight of an F-4F at St Louis on 18 May 1973. The *Luftwaffe* initially employed about ten F-4Fs in its own paint scheme but with US national insignia with the 35 TFW at George AFB, Calif., where German pilots receive Phantom training—but for better commonality with US Air Force machines, these were later replaced by German-purchased F-4Es.

The F-4F is powered by two J79-MTU-17A engines developing 17,900 lb (8,120 kg) thrust with afterburner. These are manufactured under license in Germany by Motoren Turbinen Union. The F-4F has wing leading-edge slats. It is almost identical with the F-4E except that it does not have the slotted stabilator (a standard Phantom feature from about 1968 onwards) or the seventh fuel cell, and was delivered without air-to-air refuelling capability although this has been retroactively installed. The F-4F has the internal under-fuselage Sparrow wells and the switchology (cockpit switches) for the SARH missiles but was not intended for, and does not actually carry, Sparrows. German-manufactured outer wings, after-fuselage and tail components are included in the 175 F-4Fs manufactured in St Louis between June 1973 and April 1976.

F-4G

The F-4G designation was first applied to twelve machines on the early F-4B production line which were equipped with AN/ASW-21 datalink communications equipment for automated carrier landings. First flown 23 March 1963 at St Louis as McAir ship 269 (150481), with Thomas G Harris and John J Kiely on board in the first two-man 'first flight,' the F-4G served in combat with the 'Black Lions' of VF-213 aboard *Kitty Hawk* (CVA-63) in Vietnamese waters in the spring of 1966 and, for a time, were camouflaged in an experimental green paint scheme which the Navy ultimately chose not to adopt. The twelve F-4Gs are included in the total of 651 F-4Bs built and all returned to the F-4B configuration.

F-4G

The F-4G designation was trotted out a second time for the US Air Force's current Advanced Wild Weasel electronic warfare aircraft, a converted F-4E. Initial tests were conducted with McAir ship 1761 (65-713), a modified F-4D, while the first actual F-4G flown was McAir ship 3932 (69-7254) on 6 December 1975. All F-4G aircraft have their J79-GE-17 engines modified to render them 'smokeless,' eliminating the telltale visual track of earler Phantoms.

Hard lessons from North Vietnam and from the October 1973 Middle East war highlighted the need for a tactical aircraft designed to 'take out' enemy ground missile installations. Heart of the F-4G is the McDonnell Douglas AN/APR-38 radar and missile detection and launch homing system, rigged to 52 antennas in nose, amidships and in tail positions. This 'black box' is reprogrammable at squadron level and capable of identifying all Warsaw Pact radar systems currently known and of displaying their locations in a predetermined

The F-4G, Air Force Advanced Wild Weasel. A converted F-4E with electronics gear in the nose fairing once intended for a 20-mm. cannon, the F-4G is easily distinguished by the fairing at the tip of the vertical tail surface. F-4G Phantom 69-7566 of the 81st Tactical Fighter Squadron, 52nd Tactical Fighter Wing, coded SP, based at Spangdahlem AB, Germany as part of the American commitment to NATO, is seen visiting RAF Wethersfield, England in 1983

order of priority to the crew. To engage enemy sensors, the F-4G carries anti-radar weapons such as the AGM-45 Shrike, AGM-78 standard ARM and AGM-88 HARM (High-speed Anti-Radiation Missile); guided weapons such as the AGM-65 Maverick (primarily D models with IR thermal imaging sensors) and Mk 84 electro-optical guided bombs (EOGB) as well as cluster weapons such as Rockeye, CBU-52 and CBU-58.

For its own defense, although the 20-mm cannon has been deleted, the F-4G carries jammer pods, AN/ALE-40 chaff and IR flare dispensers, AIM-7F Sparrow SARH and AIM-9L Sidewinder air-to-air missiles.

The F-4G reached initial operating capability with the 37 Tactical Fighter Wing under Col Gene Thweatt at George AFB, California in October 1978. Other units employing the Advanced Wild Weasel are the 52 TFW at Spangdahlem AB, Germany and the 3 TFW at Clark AB, Philippines.

YF-4J

In anticipation of the US Navy's F-4J program, three existing F-4B airframes were converted to YF-4J standard to test systems for the new model. The first of these, McAir ship 550 (151473) made its first flight on 4 June 1976. The aircraft remained in service for some years and were used in various Navy test programs.

F-4J

The *second* F-4J airframe buiit, McAir ship 1506

(153072) was the first of this major US Navy variant to fly, at St Louis on 27 May 1966. The first F-4J, McAir ship 1488 (153071) has been a fixture at NAS Patuxent River, Maryland for many years.

To achieve more flexible carrier operations, landing gross weight was increased in the F-4J and the aircraft was designed to approach at lower speeds. This was done by introducing drooped ailerons and slotted stabilator, the latter (mentioned in the section on the F-4F) widely credited as a British invention, permitting improved performance at high angles of attack on carrier approaches. The F-4J was equipped with APQ-59 radar with 32-inch (81 cm) dish and AWF-10 pulse-doppler fire control system which permits the detection and tracking of high and low altitude targets. The F-4J also incorporated space provisions for the AN/ASW-25A datalink landing system originally flown on the Navy F-4G. It had improved TACAN and an upgraded AN/AJB-7 bombing system as well as APR-32 radar homing and early warning system (RHAWS). The J model is powered by J79-GE-19 engines with 17,900 lb (8,120 kg) thrust with afterburning. Approach speed has been reduced from 137 to 125 knots

(253 km/h to 231 km/h) with the installation of drooped ailerons.

The F-4J played a major role in combat over North Vietnam. A few were in action in time to participate in Rolling Thunder operations which ended in October 1968. F-4Js returned to North Vietnam in the 1972 Linebacker campaign to produce the Navy's only aces. Marine Corps F-4Js were the last American aircraft in operation in Southeast Asia, departing Nam Phong, Thailand in August 1973.

522 aircraft were built between September 1966 and December 1971. Actual delivery of the last F-4J took place 7 January 1972. Fifteen were

BELOW
The F-4J. The 'Ghostriders' of VF-142 were the first Phantom squadron in combat. Here, an F-4J Phantom of theirs (155875) carrying a standard centerline tank and with full flaps down, lands aboard USS Enterprise (CVAN-65) in the Indian Ocean in 1972. On 26 April 1973, still with the same squadron and ship, this F-4J suffered an in-flight fire and was lost at sea after the crew ejected
(US Navy)

scheduled to be transferred from the US Navy to the Royal Air Force in October 1984. At least one machine was converted into a DF-4J drone controller. 302 airframes had been scheduled for conversion to F-4S standard but the program ended with 248 having been so modified.

F-4J Phantom (153792) of the 'Red Devils' of Marine squadron VMFA-232 at MCAS El Toro, California in March 1968, soon to depart for Vietnam. 'Red Devils' were the last American combat unit to leave Southeast Asia, departing the 'Rose Garden' at Nam Phong, Thailand—the only airbase not located near sea from which Marine aviation has gone to war—in August 1974 (Duane A Kasulka)

DF-4J

Late in its service life, the F-4J entered use as a drone control aircraft at the Naval Missile Center, Point Mugu, California, one example being McAir ship 1643 (153084), which was noted with the DF-4J designation in August 1983.

YF-4K

First flown 27 June 1966, two service test aircraft for the Royal Navy (XT595 and XT596) came before production of that service's F-4K model.

F-4K

First flown on 2 November 1966, the F-4K was built for the Royal Navy with raised nose gear, slotted stabilator, Rolls Royce 202/203 engines, and other design changes. After the Royal Navy ceased using carriers which could handle the Phantom, the 50 airplanes of this variant were transferred to the Royal Air Force.

YF-4M

First flown on 17 February 1967, two service-test

aircraft for the Royal Air Force came ahead of production of the RAF's F-4M model. These two machines (XT852 and XT853) tested systems for the F-4M model.

F-4M

First flown 26 December 1967, no fewer than 116 F-4M Phantoms were built for the RAF. British Phantoms of the YF-4K, F-4K, YF-4M and F-4M series are treated exhaustively in a companion volume in the Osprey Air Combat series, *McDonnell Douglas F-4K and F-4M Phantom II*, by Michael Burns (London: Osprey Publishing Limited, 1984).

F-4N

A rebuild of the F-4B, the F-4N Phantom reflects the US Navy's favourable experience with a Service Life Extension Program (SLEP) first tried on variants of the Vought F-8 Crusader and later employed with success converting F-4J airframes to F-4S standard. This update program was carried out by the Naval Air Rework Facility (NARF) at NAS North Island, California, near

The F-4J. The 'Aardvarks' of VF-114 were an early
Phantom squadron and used both the F-4B and F-4J in
combat against North Vietnam. These F-4Js were caught
by McDonnell Douglas's Harry Gann over California just
after hostilities in 1974. Plane in background (157267) was
serving with 'Fighting Falcons' of VF-96 when flown by
Navy aces Lt Randy Cunningham and Lt (jg) Willie
Driscoll for their first two MiG kills—a MiG on 19
January 1972, and a MiG-17 on May 8th
(MDC)

BELOW
The F-4G (See page 101). During combat operations over
South Vietnam from Dixie Station in July 1965, F-4G
datalink Phantom (150636), coded as NH-107 of the
'Black Lions' of VF-213 makes a landing on the USS
Kitty Hawk (CVA-63) in the South China Sea. The
twelve F-4G Phantoms were outwardly no different in
appearance than the F-4B model, an example of which is
depicted at right with a full load of bombs for strikes
against the Viet Cong
(James T Sullivan)

Royal Navy markings, Royal Air Force camouflage. This combination of markings on F-4K-36-MC serial XV579, is explained by the RAF lending a number of FG.1s to the RN for training purposes. The diving gull insignia of No 767 Sqn, Fleet Air Arm, is visible on the fin (Paul Bennett)

An F-4N Phantom (151016) of the 'Fighting Vigilantes' of VF-151 makes a 1976 launch from the last carrier to operate Phantoms, the USS Midway (CVA-41) (AQ1 Stephen Daniels)

Royal Air Force Phantom F-4Ms (FGR.2s) in weathered, gray, low-visibility air defence scheme with small muted 'pink and lilac' roundels. Both these machines XV412/'H' (nearest) and XV485/'W' were previously on the strength of No 23 Sqn, but the 'Fortress Falklands' shake-up saw them transferred to No 29 Sqn based at Coningsby, Lincolnshire, in England. Interestingly, both aircraft sport a different variation of the No 29 Sqn badge insignia 'H' is equipped with a RWR (Radar Warning Receiver) and ILS (Instrument Landing System) antennae on the fin, a configuration now standard on RAF Phantoms. Picture taken in 1983 (Norman Pealing)

San Diego, beginning in 1971 under Profject Bee Line. First flight was made on 4 June 1972 by McAir ship 1574 (153034). The F-4N has an improved structure and updated equipment items such as the helmet-sight Visual Target Acquisition System (VTAS), Sidewinder Expanded Acquisition Mode (SEAM), improved computer, and one-way datalink. Old F-4Bs from blocks 12 through 28 were converted to F-4N, a total of 228 in all, and also received new block numbers.

QF-4N

Forty QF-4N drones are being created by converting F-4N airframes. A report dated 11 February 1984 indicated that the program had slipped far behind schedule with only two machines, 150630 and 151004, then converted. The first of these (150630) flown by Lt Cdr Kenneth L Buchspics, project pilot, was unveiled at the Naval Missile Center, Point Mugu,

California in February 1983. The QF-4N has the full manoeuvring capability lacking in the QF-4B. Clark W McCay, project manager, says the QF-4N 'is the most effective simulation of a real threat yet developed.'

F-4P

Apparently to compensate Israel for its refusal to export the Martin RB-57F high-altitude reconnaissance aircraft, the US Air Force and General Dynamics in the mid-1970s jointly embarked on programs aimed at producing a Phantom reconnaissance aircraft capable of operating as high as 76,000 ft (23,170 m), or above the performance envelope of the MiG-25 Foxbat. Under the Peace Jack program, at least one F-4E (69-7576) was modified to carry the General Dynamics HIAC camera of 66-in focal length operating through side and bottom-mounted oblique windows, altering the nose shape and increasing fuselage length by 12 in (304.5 mm). 69-7576 operated at Edwards AFB in 1976 with Israeli desert camouflage and US markings. An Israeli-developed Elta jamming system may also have been among its equipment. 69-7576 was later 'mocked up' with external tanks which fattened the fuselage shape and were designed to hold *water*—to give the aircraft water-injected boost speed. Various other designations, including RF-4(X), RF-4E(S) and F-4X have been quoted unofficially either for the 69-7576 testbed or for proposed developments. The water-injection

system was apparently never tested or used, and no further details have come to light except that the Edwards test machine was designated F-4P.

F-4S

The F-4S entered Marine Corps and Fleet service as part of a Service Life Extension Program (SLEP) similar to the one which produced the F-4N from existing F-4B airframes. First flown 22 July 1977, the first example being McAir ship 4119 (158360) and tested extensively at NAS Patuxent River, Maryland, the F-4S has increased structural strength, longer fatigue life, and a new AN/AGW-10A radar which has necessitated retraining for RIOs. The US Navy reports that the F-4S requires 25 per cent less maintenance time than the F-4J, an important improvement for a complex and sophisticated fighter type. The F-4S' J79-GE-10B engines are smokeless.

Beginning in September 1979, the 47th and subsequent F-4S conversions include the McDonnell Douglas two-position leading edge manoeuvre wing slat, while the first 47 F-4Ss were to have slats retrofitted. The Navy was thus almost

The F-4S. Shown in the 'low visibility' camouflage scheme which has been standard in the 1980s, this F-4S Phantom (157245), coded DW-02, belonging to the 'Thunderbolts' of Marine squadron VMFA-251 was photographed at NAS Oceana, Virginia on 30 April 1983. The F-4S can be distinguished by the formation lights which appear as a thin, sweptback strip on the tail and a narrow strip on the side of the fuselage above the wing leading edge (Don Linn)

a decade behind the Air Force in introducing slats, although it had tested fixed leading edge slats at Patuxent on one F-4J Phantom (153088), a machine which is better known for having been painted in a colourful bicentennial scheme during the 200th anniversary of American independence in 1976.

The F-4S can be visually identified by the Air Force-style formation strip lights (used by the latter service since the late 1960s) on the vertical stabilizer and above the wing along the fuselage.

248 F-4Js (of 302 once planned) were converted to F-4S standard. First deliveries went to the Marine Corps beginning with the Beaufort, South Carolina-based 'Warlords' of VMFA-451 under Lt Col R N Patrick. The 'Lancers' of VMFA-212 at Kaneohe Bay, Hawaii, second to receive the F-4S, were first to deploy, taking their aircraft to MCAS Iwakuni, Japan in October 1979 for a six-month TDY (temporary duty). With the USS *Midway* (CVA-41) now the only aircraft carrier operating Phantoms, the F-4S aircraft of the 'Vigilantes' of VF-151 and the 'Chargers' of VF-161 are now the only regularly operational carrier-based Phantoms in the world.

F-4T

Before the corporate decision that the future did not call for 'Phantoms forever,' McDonnell engineers began preliminary work on an advanced Phantom design with the designation F-4T. The proposal was virtually nipped in the bud and not even early design studies were completed.

Table 4–1. F-4C Aircraft converted to Wild Weasel

The following F-4C Phantoms were converted to 'Wild Weasel' electronic warfare duties and are known, at least informally, as EF-4C.

No.	Block	Serials
4	F-4C-16-MC	63-7423, 63-7433, 63-7437, 63-7440
6	F-4C-17-MC	63-7443, 63-7447, 63-7452, 63-7459, 63-7462, 63-7467
7	F-4C-18-MC	63-7470, 63-7474, 63-7478, 63-7481, 63-7508, 63-7512, 63-7513
6	F-4C-19-MC	63-7564, 63-7567, 63-7568, 63-7574, 63-7594, 63-7596
2	F-4C-20-MC	63-7607, 63-7615
1	F-4C-22-MC	64-675
7	F-4C-23-MC	64-741, 64-757, 64-781, 64-787, 64-790, 64-791, 64-815
3	F-4C-24-MC	64-840, 64-844, 64-847

36 Total

Table 4–2. F-4 aircraft equipped with AN/ARN-92 LORAN

The AN/ARN-92 long range navigation system (LORAN) was developed to suit combat conditions in Southeast Asia, where aircraft flew long sorties from bases in Thailand to targets in North Vietnam. The twenty RF-4Cs manufactured with the system and the seventy-one F-4Ds retrofitted with it had a distinctive 'towel rack' sensor on the upper rear of the fuselage. Some of these aircraft have subsequently had the system removed.

Number	Block	From	To
20	RF-4C-40-MC	68-594	68-611
—			
20	Subtotal		
7	F-4D-32-MC	66-8708	66-8714
1		66-8719	
1		66-8722	
3		66-8726	66-8728
6		66-8730	66-8735
3		66-8737	66-8739
2		66-8741	66-8742
2		66-8744	66-8745
4		66-8747	66-8750
2		66-8755	66-8756
2		66-8758	66-8759
2		66-8761	66-8762
1		66-8765	
3		66-8768	66-8770
1		66-8772	
1		66-8774	
2		66-8776	66-8777
1		66-8779	
1		66-8782	
3		66-8784	66-8786
—			
48	Subtotal		
13	F-4D-33-MC	66-8787	66-8799
2		66-8802	66-8803
2		66-8805	66-8806
1		66-8810	
2		66-8812	66-8813
1		66-8816	
1		66-8818	
1		66-8825	
—			
23	Subtotal		
71	Subtotal F-4Ds		

Table 4–3. F-4B aircraft converted to QF-4B

44 F-4B Phantoms were converted at the Naval Air Development Center (NADC), Warminster, Pennsylvania, into QF-4B drones for use at the

Naval Missile Center, Point Mugu, California, and other locations. Of these, 21 airframes have been identified by number. These are listed below.

No	Old Block Number	Bureau Numbers
4	F-4B-6-MC	148365, 148378, 148383, 148386
11	F-4B-8-MC	148393, 148415, 148424, 149409, 149414, 149420, 149428, 149431, 149432, 149433, 149434
6	F-4B-11-MC	149441, 149451, 149452, 149461, 149466, 149471

21 Total

Table 4–4. F-4J aircraft converted to F-4S

The Service Life Extension Program (SLEP) under which existing F-4J airframes were converted to F-4S standard ended with the conversion of 248 individual aircraft. These are listed below.

Number	Old Block Number	Bureau Numbers
1	F-4J-28-MC	153779
6	F-4J-29-MC	153780, 153784, 153787, 153791, 153792, 153798
19	F-4J-30-MC	153800, 153805, 153808, 153809, 153810, 153814, 153818, 153819, 153820, 153821, 153823, 153824, 153825, 153826, 153827, 153828, 153832, 153833, 153835
20	F-4J-31-MC	153840, 153842, 153843, 153845, 153847, 153851, 153853, 153855, 153856, 153857, 153858, 153859, 153860, 153862, 153864, 153868, 153869, 153872, 153873, 153874
25	F-4J-32-MC	153877, 153879, 153880, 153881, 153882, 153884, 153887, 153889, 153890, 153891, 153893, 153896, 153898, 153899, 153900, 153902, 153903, 153904, 153907, 153909, 153910, 153911, 154781, 154782
29	F-4J-33-MC	154786, 154788, 155515, 155517, 155518, 155519, 155521, 155522, 155524, 155525, 155527, 155528, 155530, 155531, 155532, 155539, 155541, 155542, 155543, 155544, 155545, 155547, 155549, 155550, 155552, 155555, 155558, 155559, 155560
40	F-4J-34-MC	155561, 155562, 155565, 155566, 155567, 155568, 155570, 155572, 155573, 155575, 155579, 155572, 155573, 155575, 155579, 155731, 155732, 155733, 155735, 155736, 155739, 155740, 155741, 155743, 155745, 155746, 155747, 155749, 155753, 155754, 155757, 155759, 155761, 155764, 155765, 155766, 155767, 155769, 155772, 155773, 155779, 155781, 155783, 155784
28	F-4J-35-MC	155786, 155787, 155792, 155794, 155801, 155805, 155806, 155807, 155808, 155810, 155812, 155813, 155818, 155820, 155821, 155822, 155823, 155825, 155827, 155828, 155829, 155830, 155833, 155834, 155836, 155838, 155839, 155840
12	F-4J-36-MC	155845, 155847, 155848, 155849, 155851, 155854, 155855, 155858, 155859, 155862,

Number	Old Block Number	Bureau Numbers
		155863, 155864
4	F-4J-37-MC	155869, 155871, 155872, 155874
7	F-4J-38-MC	155876, 155878, 155879, 155881, 155883, 155887, 155888
10	F-4J-39-MC	155890, 155891, 155892, 155893, 155896, 155897, 155898, 155899, 155900, 155901
12	F-4J-40-MC	157242, 157243, 157245, 157246, 157248, 157249, 157250, 157254, 157255, 157257, 157259, 157260
4	F-4J-41-MC	157267, 157268, 157269, 157272
6	F-4J-42-MC	157276, 157278, 157279, 157281, 157282, 157283
7	F-4J-43-MC	157287, 157290, 157291, 157292, 157293, 157296, 157297
7	F-4J-44-MC	157298, 157301, 157304, 157305, 157307, 157308, 157309
6	F-4J-45-MC	158346, 158348, 158350, 158352, 158353, 158354
1	F-4J-46-MC	158362
4	F-4J-47-MC	158370, 158372, 158374, 158376

248 Total

Table 4–5. F-4B aircraft converted to F-4N

As part of a Service Life Extension Program (SLEP) called Project Beeline, 228 F-4B Phantoms were converted to F-4N standard. These are listed below.

F-4N Block	Prod Seq	Serial Number	F-4B Block
R&D	FP02	153034	27
	P001	150430	12
	P002	150652	15
1	P003	150491	14
	P004	150452	13
	P005	150635	14

F-4N Block	Prod Seq	Serial Number	F-4B Block
	P006	150444	13
	P007	151398	15
2	P008	150460	13
	P009	151424	16
	P010	150407	12
	P011	150634	14
	P012	150441	13
3	P013	151016	14
	P014	151451	18
	P015	150422	12
	P016	151491	19
	P017	150996	15
4	P018	151015	15
	P019	150445	13
	P020	150472	13
	P021	151433	17
	P022	151442	17
5	P023	151434	17
	P024	151006	15
	P025	151400	16
	P026	150425	12
	P027	150479	13
6	P028	150640	14
	P029	150627	14
	P030	150450	13
	P031	150485	14
	P032	150625	14
7	P033	152235	21
	P034	152267	22
	P035	150466	13
	P036	151439	17
	P037	152241	21
8	P038	151480	19
	P039	150412	12
	P040	151004	15
	P041	152291	23
	P042	151431	17
9	P043	150630	14
	P044	152280	23
	P045	150411	12
	P046	152230	21
	P047	150651	14
10	P048	150468	13
	P049	151513	20
	P050	151468	18
	P051	151435	17
	P052	150648	14
11	P053	150429	12
	P054	151459	18
	P055	151417	16

F-4N Block	Prod Seq	Serial Number	F-4B Block	F-4N Block	Prod Seq	Serial Number	F-4B Block
	P056	151476	19		P106	150426	12
	P057	151463	18		P107	150638	14
12	P058	150492	14	22	P108	152969	25
	P059	152278	23		P109	153024	26
	P060	151519	20		P110	152967	25
	P061	150482	14		P111	152227	21
	P062	150475	13		P112	151502	20
13	P063	151484	19	23	P113	151498	20
	P064	150476	13		P114	151422	16
	P065	152277	23		P115	150478	13
	P066	150465	13		P116	152237	21
	P067	151430	17		P117	152210	20
14	P068	151469	18	24	P118	153059	28
	P069	150642	14		P119	153047	27
	P070	151456	18		P120	151464	18
	P071	151436	17		P121	150432	12
	P072	152306	24		P122	150481	14
15	P073	151000	15	25	P123	153026	26
	P074	151444	17		P124	151401	16
	P075	151448	18		P125	153045	27
	P076	150436	13		P126	153065	28
	P077	152259	22		P127	150464	13
16	P078	152258	22	26	P128	152977	25
	P079	152272	22		P129	151475	19
	P080	152253	22		P130	152318	24
	P081	151489	19		P131	152281	23
	P082	152229	21		P132	153053	27
17	P083	150419	12	27	P133	152295	23
	P084	152288	23		P134	153039	27
	P085	150643	13		P135	153050	27
	P086	150438	13		P136	153023	26
	P087	151413	16		P137	152975	25
18	P088	150456	13	28	P138	153914	28
	P089	150448	13		P139	152981	25
	P090	150632	14		P140	153017	26
	P091	150423	12		P141	152252	22
	P092	151406	16		P142	152313	24
19	P093	152254	22	29	P143	152323	24
	P094	152236	21		P144	151514	20
	P095	150415	12		P145	151452	18
	P096	150489	14		P146	151477	19
	P097	151003	15		P147	150480	14
20	P098	152294	23	30	P148	150440	13
	P099	152302	23		P149	153008	26
	P100	151471	18		P150	152982	25
	P101	152991	25		P151	151446	17
	P102	152223	21		P152	153016	26
21	P103	152275	23	31	P153	152293	23
	P104	150442	13		P154	150639	14
	P105	151487	19		P155	151008	15

*Gerald 'Zeke' Huelsbeck, who had flown Banshees and
Demons, was the McDonnell test pilot killed in the crash
near Edwards AFB, California of the first Phantom,
F4H-1 142259. Note Huelbeck's pressure helmet, the same
as that of Mercury astronauts
(MDC)*

F4H-1 Phantom 146817, the 19th aircraft built, was used for Sparrow missile tests at NAS Patuxent River, Maryland. The aircraft is seen here in July 1960 carrying six AIM-7 Sparrows
(MDC)

BELOW
F4H-1 Phantom 143391, the sixth airframe built, was flown by Cdr Paul Spencer in carrier qualification tests. Here, number six is readied for launch from 78,700-ton USS Independence (CVA-62) off the Atlantic coast in April 1960
(MDC)

Specially painted for the May 1961 Project LANA cross-country speed run, F4H-1 Phantom 148266, soon to be redesignated F-4A, belonged to Detachment A of the 'Grim Reapers' of VF-101 (coded AD-182) when it was photographed preparing for the trans-American speed dash (MDC)

BELOW
*The US Air Force thought its Phantom would be the F-110A, but the designation was painted only on Navy F-4B 149405, borrowed for evaluation. The same machine depicted on the front cover, 149405 is seen in St Louis snow with a non-standard green anti-glare shield in January 1962
(MDC)*

OPPOSITE
*In April 1964, the 12th and 15th Tactical Fighter Wings
were working up in the Phantom at MacDill AFB,
Florida. Photo shows a mix of F-4Cs including 63-7418
(foreground) and borrowed Navy F-4Bs
(MDC)*

BOTTOM RIGHT
*En route to North Vietnam. F-4C Phantom 64-708, with
63-7668 in background, from different 'Wolfpack'
squadrons, head north on a Rolling Thunder mission
carrying 750 lb (340 kg) bombs
(Frank MacSorley)*

BELOW
*Combat. Showing the severe weathering of early
camouflage paint, F-4C Phantom 633-7556 of the 433rd
Tactical Fighter Squadron, 8th Tactical Fighter Wing—
Col Robin Olds' 'Wolfpack'—on a combat mission in
Southeast Asia
(Frank MacSorley)*

Marine RF-4B Phantom 153099 wears one-of-a-kind
paint scheme tried by squadron VMFP-3 but not adopted
on an afternoon simulated carrier launch at MCAS El
Toro, California on 21 August 1975
(US Marine Corps)

TOP LEFT
'Peanut Butter Crackers' is the nickname on the splitter
vane of RF-4C Phantom 65-863 from the 11th Tactical
Reconnaissance Squadron carrying sharktoothed centreline
tank on a combat mission over Vietnam in about 1969.
Note the exposed chaff/flare dispenser on the rear fuselage
(Frank MacSorley)

Two F-4N Phantoms of Reserve Squadron VF-301, the
'Devil's Disciples', fly over USS Ranger (CV-61) in 1977.
Aircraft in foreground, 150456, before being converted
from F-4B to F-4N, shot down a North Vietnamese MiG-
17 on 6 May 1972
(US Navy)

Dorsal fuel receptacle opened, RF-4C Phantom 72-153
callsign ZEROX 53 of the 26th Tactical Reconnaissance
Wing, Zwiebrucken AB, West Germany, closes in on
Boeing KC-135 Stratotanker 59-1461, callsign DOBBY
32, of the 8th Air Refuelling Squadron, on a mission over
Germany on 24 May 1984
(Robert F Dorr)

F-4N Block	Prod Seq	Serial Number	F-4B Block	F-4N Block	Prod Seq	Serial Number	F-4B Block
	P156	152243	21	42	P206	151002	15
	P157	153915	28		P207	152290	23
32	P158	152226	21		P208	152246	22
	P159	151510	20		P209	151449	18
	P160	152221	21		P210	151455	18
	P161	151440	17	43	P211	152971	25
	P162	152222	21		P212	153064	28
33	P163	152326	24		P213	150490	14
	P164	153058	26		P214	152992	25
	P165	153012	26		P215	152303	20
	P166	152968	25		P216	152279	23
	P167	152965	25	44	P217	150628	14
34	P168	151504	20		P218	151007	15
	P169	153067	28		P219	152217	21
	P170	152225	24		P220	151011	15
	P171	152310	24		P221	150484	14
	P172	152214	20		P222	153006	26
35	P173	152317	27	45	P223	151482	19
	P174	152970	30		P224	152327	24
	P175	153010	26		P225	151511	20
	P176	152212	20		P226	152284	23
	P177	152250	20	46	P227	153034	
36	P178	150435	12				
	P179	152208	20				
	P180	153056	27				
	P181	152269	22				
	P182	152996	26				
37	P183	152282	23				
	P184	151415	16				
	P185	150993	15				
	P186	151465	18				
	P187	152307	24				
38	P188	152300	23				
	P189	152283	22				
	P190	152983	25				
	P191	153036	27				
	P192	153057	28				
39	P193	152270	22				
	P194	152990	25				
	P195	152298	23				
	P196	152244	22				
	P197	153019	26				
40	P198	153027	26				
	P199	152986	25				
	P200	153062	28				
	P201	153030	27				
	P202	153011	26				
41	P203	151503	20				
	P204	151461	18				
	P205	152321	24				

Chapter 5
Rematch

May 10th, 1972: The Killing of Colonel Tomb

When the last Phantom has gone to the final boneyard, men will still speak of the great air battles of 10 May 1972. It was, for the Phantom, the longest day. It was a day like no other for men from Udorn, from Ubon, from Yankee Station...

For Capt Donald S Pickard, the day began with an early-morning motorcycle ride from the 14th Tactical Reconnaissance Squadron's billets to the 432nd Wing's briefing room at Udorn. Pickard, the young sailor of page 34, had gone to college, had earned an Air Force commission, and had flown RF-101 Voodoos before graduating into the RF-4C. He was a sturdy, drawling southerner. 'The briefing room was *packed*! There were huge target maps of the Hanoi rail yard and the Doumer Bridge. Everybody knew we were going back at last.'

The 432nd commander, Col Charles A Gabriel, looked gaunt and serious. Maj Robert N Lodge, operations officer, was talking up the mission with the others—a spirited, natural leader. Lodge would lead OYSTER flight of four F-4Ds from the wing's 'Triple Nickel' 555 TFS—and was now well into the final hours of his life. A two-plane reconnaissance RF-4C element, FALCON flight, consisting of Maj Sidney Rogers, Don Pickard, and their back-seaters would be flying post-strike recce over Hanoi's Yen Bien rail yards and the Doumer Bridge. Pickard would arrive in the middle of Route Package Six long after North Vietnam's defences were alerted and zeroed-in.

At Ubon, the briefing room was packed, too. The 8th Tactical Fighter Wing's 'Wolfpack,' under Col Carl S Miller would attack the Yen Bien marshalling complex and the Paul Doumer Bridge. Both were just outside Hanoi and critical to the capital and the enemy's war effort. Two flights of F-4Ds dropping chaff to foil enemy radar would be followed by a 16-plane attack force

in flights of four F-4Es each. JINGLE, NAPKIN and BILOXI flights would carry Mark 84 2,000-lb (908-kg) laser-guided bombs. GOATEE flight would carry electro-optical guided bombs (EOGB).

Captain Thomas (Mike) Messett listened to the briefing and pondered. Messett thought back to how things had been in the first campaign over the North. During Rolling Thunder, Messett had been a back-seater on an August 1967 strike against the Doumer Bridge—the all-too-familiar trestle span which was the brunt of an obscene song by fighter pilots—when anti-aircraft fire exploded around his Phantom and wounded the flier up front. Messett took control of the damaged aircraft, dropped its bombs, and made a difficult save of the Phantom with emergency in-flight refuelling and a back-seat landing at Ubon. Now a front-seat pilot himself, flying once more against the Doumer Bridge, known properly as the Hanoi Highway and Railway Bridge, Mike Messett would be returning to settle a grudge.

At 0800, the chaff bombers were airborne. At 0820, Mike Messett hauled back on his stick and his heavily-laden F-4E Phantom bounded aloft.

Thus, MiGCAP and post-strike recce came from Udorn while chaff- and bomb-carrying Phantoms rose from Ubon. This illustrates a division of responsibility which had not existed during Rolling Thunder when, as Messett says, 'everybody was doing everything.' Already the air-to-ground fighter of the war, the Phantom had replaced the F-105 as the principal weapon in the air-to-ground strike role. Duties were compartmentalized, the 432 TRW at Udorn being assigned the air-to-air function while the 8 TFW at Ubon carried ordnance. Today, they would be accompanied into the hotly-contested Hanoi/Haiphong area by four EB-66s for ECM

TOP
The Wolfpack at war. F-4D Phantom (66-234) of the 8th Tactical Fighter Wing carrying AIM-7F Sparrows, ECM pods and Mk 84 2,000-lb (908-kg) laser-guided bombs during combat operations against North Vietnam (US Air Force)

ABOVE
Although this is one of the earliest photos of an F-4E model Phantom in combat taken 1 January 1969 during the period between bombing campaigns over North Vietnam, Phantom 67-299 of the 469th Tactical Fighter Squadron, 388th Tactical Fighter Wing (JV) based at Korat AB, Thailand, already looks war-weary. The serial number is hastily and incompletely painted on the tail. Aircraft carries an ECM device on inboard pylon and only one small bomb in the outboard position, indicating that it is on an electronic mission (US Air Force)

Typical of other aircraft over North Vietnam during the stepped-up attacks of 10 May 1972 was Vought A-7E Corsair (157537) of attack squadron VA-192 from the USS Kitty Hawk (CVA-63). While Phantoms covered them, A-7Es carried 1,000-lb (454 kg) Mark 83 bombs against the Hai Duoung rail yard complex. Lt Cdr Norman D Campbell, flying an A-7E in sister squadron VA-195, was narrowly missed by a SAM missile (US Navy)

OPPOSITE PAGE
May 10th MiG killers. Taken the day before the biggest air-to-air battles over North Vietnam, photo shows deck of USS Constellation crammed with Vigilantes, Corsairs, Phantoms. Phantom closest to camera, coded NG-106, is F-4J 155769, which shot down two MiG-17s on 10 May 1972 while flown by Lt Michael J Connelly and Lt Thomas J J Blonski. Farther back, coded NG-110, is F-4J 155779 which was regularly assigned to Lt Randall H Cunningham and Lt (jg) William P Driscoll, although they scored none of their five MiG kills in it (US Navy)

support, fifteen F-105Gs for SAM suppression, and a further sixteen F-4E Phantoms with unguided 500-lb (227-kg) bombs—these from the 388 TFW at Korat. It was a massive effort, staging so many Air Force missions out of several bases in Thailand. They would refuel in flight and ingress North Vietnam through the 'Gorilla's Head' on the Laotian border.

Far to the northeast, the attack carriers *Constellation* and *Coral Sea* began to launch, with *Kitty Hawk* soon to follow—an unprecedented armada of three carrier air wings. While the force from Thailand drove into his airspace, the enemy would confront an assault from the other direction, from the Gulf of Tonkin, where the carrier strike force took to the sky. The Navy would attack targets around Haiphong and had also been given its own rail yard and bridge—both named Hai Duong. . .

In October 1968, Lyndon Johnson had ended Operation Rolling Thunder and cleansed North Vietnamese skies of US aircraft. In 1971, Richard Nixon had authorized 'limited duration, protective

Heading for targets in North Vietnam. During the Linebacker campaign, an F-4J Phantom 157252 of the 'Aardvarks' of fighter squadron VF-114, coded NH-203 and loaded with ordnance, heads in the general direction of Hanoi. VF-114's aircraft scored several MiG kills (US Navy)

Tailhook catching the wire, F-4J Phantom of the 'Silver Kites' of VF-92 lands on USS Constellation (CVA-64) in the South China Sea in July 1974 (US Navy)

reaction' air strikes during Operation Proud Deep—a limited return to the North, with severe constraints on geography, ordnance and targets. Two days ago, May 8th, Nixon had announced the bombing of Haiphong harbour. Today, 10 May 1972, was the outset of the second major campaign against North Vietnam—Linebacker, it would be called, destined to be very different from Rolling Thunder. This time, all the stops were off.

It must be assumed that Col Tomb briefed his fighter pilots on this morning, too. Soviet-trained, equipped with 300-odd MiG-17, MiG-19 and MiG-21 fighters, North Vietnam's pilots were part of a massive air defence network which included radar, ground control intercept (GCI), SAM and AAA sites. Seven fighter bases lay around the Hanoi-Haiphong region. Tomb's pilots could be in battle in minutes, did not need to carry external fuel, did not need to refuel in flight, and could choose the time and place of any engagement with the approaching Phantom force. While history often favours he who attacks, in this instance all of the advantages lay with the defender.

A pair of US Navy F-4J Phantoms of VF-92 from *Constellation* (CVA-64) stirred up enemy defences first and may have provoked MiG action against the later strikes of the day. These F-4Js were assigned as MiG combat air patrol (MiGCAP) for the first Navy strikes of the day on POL storage near Haiphong. They chanced upon a pair of heavily-laden MiG-21s climbing out after take-off from Kep—and pounced. The time was 0950. Lt Curt Dose and Lt Cdr James McDevitt in F-4J Phantom 157269, coded NG-211, callsign SILVER KITE 211, shot down one MiG with a pair of Sidewinders. The other MiG pilot had no wish to be aggressive. He scurried off and eluded the MiGCAP force.

For three and a half years, no American warplanes had been seen or heard over downtown Hanoi. On the ground, American prisoners interpreted the long silence as proof they had been abandoned. Now, for the first time in all those years, they heard AAA guns booming and reverberating in the city. The time was 1015. There was an 85-mm AAA battery across the street from the prison which now began firing with thunderous volume. Guards poked and prodded the men into the centre of the windowless room where they could not see *why* guns resounded.

Maj Kenneth W Cordier, last encountered on page 60, eluded the guards. Ken struggled to the latrine where there was a small high window and attempted to raise himself high enough to see out. Not even aware that he was a major, promoted while in captivity, Ken Cordier fought his way upward in the cramped, urine-smelling room, raised his chin above the window ledge, and looked up. The sounds of a great air battle boomed in his ears. Just before the guards reached him to drag him away, Ken looked up through a break in the clouds and spotted two F-4 Phantoms veering sharply over downtown Hanoi. 'They've come back!' he cried aloud. After more than half a decade in prison, after torture, after despairing that his countrymen would remember, it was the thrill of his life. *'Our guys have come back! . . .'*

Paul Doumer Bridge: Mike Messett

In successive waves, flights of the Phantom attack force arrived over the Paul Doumer Bridge and rolled in. May 10th was formally the start of the southwest monsoon season but from high altitude Mike Messett and his wingmen had an unimpeded view of the 5,532-ft (1,686-m), 19-span highway-rail bridge. The bridge was unprotected by cloud cover, although puffs of smoke from exploding 85-mm AAA shells and criss-crossing 37-mm tracers seemed to be everywhere.

Mike Messett and his flight of four Phantoms moved into a tight formation. The object was to make all four F-4Es as difficult to hit as a single aircraft. They had to maintain this formation discipline during roll-in and attack for their Mark 84 guided bombs to enter the laser 'basket'—an invisible cone of airspace, within which the bombs would guide—created by the flight leader.

Laden with bombs, F-4E Phantom (67-315) of the 388th Tactical Fighter Wing heads for Vietnamese targets in May 1970
(US Air Force)

HANOI RR/HWY BR OV RED RIVER

27 MAY 68

FLOATING CRANE

REPLACED SPANS ←

Messett watched other aircraft weaving between swirls of AAA fire and thought he saw bombs striking the bridge span. There was so much smoke from exploding ordnance that segments of the bridge were obscured. Messett's flight leader released his bombs at about 14,000 ft (4,270 m), the visual cue for the others to do the same—and Mike did. Pulling away, he was sure some of the bombs impacted the centre span of the bridge.

Cunningham and Driscoll

The Navy's next strike of the day was against the marshalling yards at Hai Duong, another rail chokepoint between Hanoi and Haiphong, protected by the defences of both cities.

Twenty-seven aircraft launched from *Constellation*. The time was 1130. The Phantoms refuelled in flight, fuel depletion being a major concern to Phantom crews at all times, and by noon they were in position for the run-in to target. Eleven F-4Js from the 'Fighting Falcons' of VF-96 were each loaded with centreline tanks, triple ejector racks carrying Mk 20 Rockeye bombs to

A key target for the Phantom attack force on 10 May 1972 was the Paul Doumer Bridge, a highway and rail trestle span at Hanoi. Bomb damage to the bridge is seen here from earlier strikes in 1968 (US Air Force)

take on North Vietnamese flak crews, and four Sidewinders. After hitting the rail yard they would provide cover for the rest of the strike group. Additional flak suppression would be provided by A-7E Corsairs with Shrike anti-radiation missiles. A-6 Intruder and A-7 Corsair strike aircraft would drop chaff to disrupt enemy radar. All did not go according to plan as the A-6 Intruders overshot the target and were obliged to roll in from the wrong direction.

The furious defences mounted by Hanoi that day are recalled by Capt David Moss from VA-94 on *Coral Sea* (CVA-43) who went in on a low-level strike at the controls of A-7E Corsair 158002, callsign HOBOKEN 601. 'An A-6 was pulling out of a dive at Hai Duong and he either took a 57-mm at the wing root or had an engine failure. First one and then the other wing came off.' This seems to refer to A-6A Intruder 155709 from

VMA-224 on *Coral Sea*, lost at about this time.
'We had been on the line since February 26.
Today they were shooting with *everything*. . .'

The F-4J Phantoms attacking Hai Duong made
their bomb run amid confusion, shells bursting
about them. As they came off the target, they were
attacked by MiGs.

Phantom 155797, coded NG-102, was hit and
downed by 85-mm AAA. Another Phantom was
damaged and chased off by persistent MiG-21s.

One Phantom pulling away from the rail yard
was SHOWTIME 100, flown by Lt Randall H
'Duke' Cunningham and Lt (jg) William P 'Irish'
Driscoll. Their F-4J Phantom 155800, coded NG-
100, was one of those assigned as the personal
mount of *Constellation*'s carrier air wing
commander, Cdr Gus Eggert, who was aloft today
in an A-7E. Normally, Cunningham and Driscoll
flew 155779, coded NG-110, though they had been
aboard 157267, coded NG-112 on two earlier
Proud Deep missions in which they'd shot down
enemy aircraft. Credited with two MiG kills (like
Bob Lodge and Roger Locher in the Air Force's
OYSTER lead), they were now attacked by a
MiG-17 which came at them from their seven
o'clock position. 'MiG-17! MiG-17!' a voice
boomed in Cunningham's earphones. The MiGs
overshot the Phantom. Cunningham tucked in
behind the North Vietnamese, lined up a
Sidewinder, and heard the growl in his phones
signifying that its IR seeker had acquired the
target. He fired. The Sidewinder leaped off its rail.
The MiG had seemed in easy range but was now
getting away fast. 'We've missed,' Cunningham
thought aloud. The time was 1350.

The Sidewinder caught up with the MiG some
2,500 ft (760 m) away. There was a quick fierce
explosion as missile and machine came together
and the MiG-17 ripped itself apart.

Minutes were ticking away, fuel being devoured,
since they'd pulled away from the target and
Cunningham and his wingmen were in the midst

*Eleven MiGs were shot down on 10 May 1972, more than
on any other day, all by Phantoms. The only victory from
the carrier* Coral Sea *(CVA-43) was a MiG-17 brought
down with a Sidewinder by F-4B Phantom 151398, coded
NL-110, callsign SCREAMING EAGLE, of squadron
VF-51, flown by Lt Kenneth L Cannon and Lt Roy A
Morris, Jr*
(Peter Mancus)

of a raging battle which, in all, was a three-hour
marathon, continuing well past 1400 hours. RED
CROWN, the surveillance ship in the Gulf, and
DISCO, the EC-121 Constellation airborne radar
station off the coast, were reporting large numbers
of fresh MiGs taking off, MiG-17s, MiG-19s,
MiG-21s, wave after wave, from Kep, from Phuc
Yen, from Yen Bai, from Bai Thueng. . .

Alone and Unarmed

Air Force RF-4C pilot Don Pickard in FALCON
2, aircraft 68-606, coded OZ, crossed the southern
neck of North Vietnam, reversed course, and
returned on a westerly run in loose formation with
FALCON lead, Sid Rogers' RF-4C, 68-604. The
recce Phantoms didn't usually operate in pairs.
Their motto was 'alone, unarmed, and unafraid.'
One pilot had been heard to joke, 'Two out of
three isn't bad, is it?' But in truth these men were
not afraid. Pilots of recce Phantoms often had
hundreds of hours' more experience than the men
in fighters.

Pickard and Rogers came back and went north
between Hanoi and Haiphong. Their radar
warning systems (RHAWS) told them they were
being stalked by North Vietnamese radar. SAM
missiles rushed up at them. Pickard had decided
long ago that if you could see it coming, you could
evade it—but the SAMs were coming in such
numbers that dodging one could easily mean flying
into another. The AAA and SAM barrages seemed
to increase when FALCON flight got almost as far
north as Kep—the outer limit of its penetration

RF-4C Phantom of the 432nd Tactical Reconnaissance Wing, on a photo-reconnaissance mission in Southeast Asia in August 1971 (US Air Force)

into enemy terrain—and turned south again. It was time to pickle off the tanks.

The moment Don Pickard jettisoned his fuel tanks, he knew something was wrong.

He hadn't felt the departing tanks bump into the airplane, although this was a mishap to which the Phantom was prone, but his fuel gauge indicated a leak and he was only now beginning his run-in on the target. He was also at the limits of distance and fuel, as far from help as you could get.

With his gauges indicating a fuel loss that defied explanation, Pickard had plenty else to occupy him. So many North Vietnamese fighters were aloft, from so many bases, that afterward it would be impossible to reconstruct how many MiGs the enemy committed to battle. MiG-17s and MiG-19s were in the air behind FALCON flight and closing fast as Don and Sid Rogers began their photo runs over the Yen Bien rail yard and the now-smoking Doumer bridge. SAMs flew around the two RF-4Cs by the *dozen* now, fired in furious barrages yet guided with disturbing accuracy.

Pilots worried most about the SAM's they couldn't see. The Phantom won accolades from pilots who had preferred single-seaters, like Don Pickard who had been more fond of the RF-101 than the RF-4C, because the Phantom provided an extra pair of eyes, a second opinion. Even without warning from a wingman, a Phantom crew often could spot the orange-red sustainer engine of an upcoming SAM, which looked like a roman candle. In 173 combat missions during which the only damage done to him was caused by his own departing fuel tanks, Capt Pickard had learned to jink the aircraft, then look for movement from the upward-rushing SAM. If the SAM moved too, it was locked on—and you had to take evasive action. Recce pilots tried to remind themselves constantly of the best rule when under missile attack: *Don't panic. . .*

In addition to SAMs, AAA explosions were everywhere. The two RF-4C pilots jinked to avoid the clutter of steel flying at them. Over his shoulder, Pickard actually *saw* a MiG-17 staying clear of these barrages but following close behind. Pickard was in the midst of his photo run, leaking fuel at an unknown rate, with everybody in North Vietnam trying to kill him.

OYSTER Flight

Intent on keeping MiGs away from strike aircraft in the area, Maj Robert N Lodge prowled the crowded and hard-fought Hanoi region leading the four F-4D Phantoms of OYSTER flight. Lodge's back-seater, Capt Roger C Locher, had been with him for eight months. The pair had previous Southeast Asia combat tours. Their F-4D Phantom 65-784, coded OY, the aircraft in which they'd teamed up for two previous MiG kills, was in superb condition and, so far, free of the radar failure which on rare instance hampered their top-scoring 'Triple Nickel' squadron. It was said that while on one was likely to become an ace in this war, if it could be done, Lodge and Locher would to it.

Lodge was told by the leader of BALTER flight, the other quartet of F-4Ds assigned to MiGCAP, that two of that flight's aircraft had aborted and the flight would be delayed. Lodge immediately decided to patrol the areas assigned to both flights—certain the MiGs would be up.

Lodge led OYSTER flight northwest from Hanoi, at low altitude and high speed, toward Yen Bai airfield. No US aircraft were north of them now, meaning that they could fire their SARH

Capt Richard S (Steve) Ritchie of the 555th Tactical
Fighter Squadron got his first MiG kill with OYSTER
flight on 10 May 1972 and went on to become the US Air
Force's first Vietnam ace with five air-to-air victories.
Ritchie has since left the Air Force and resides in Colorado
(US Air Force)

OPPOSITE PAGE
A rear-seat Weapons Systems Officer (WSO), or 'whizzo,'
Capt Charles B DeBellevue teamed up with Capt
Richard S (Steve) Ritchie in OYSTER 3, F-4D Phantom
66-7463 on 10 May 1972 to down a MiG. He became the
ranking ace of the Southeast Asia conflict with six kills.
Today, Lt Col DeBellevue is a front-seat F-4E pilot with
the 4th Tactical Fighter Wing at Seymour Johnson AFB,
North Carolina
(US Air Force)

Sparrow missiles in head-on attack without visual confirmation of the MiGs. This gave Bob Lodge a monumental advantage over the enemy's flight leader because the MiGs, with IR missiles only, had no missile designed for head-on attack.

Back-seater Locher's scope told him of numerous MiG-21 flights ahead, up at 15,000 ft (4,570 m). Lodge decided it was time to stop hugging the ground. He led OYSTER flight upstairs on afterburner. Locher achieved a radar lock-on the third of four approaching MiG-21s. Lodge prepared for a Sparrow front quartering shot, left to right. He fired a Sparrow. It started to guide toward an oncoming MiG-21 but exploded prematurely. Lodge fired again. The range was down to six miles and the missile began to guide. Lodge peered straight ahead and watched a red-orange blast consume the MiG and hurl debris in all directions.

OYSTER 2, F-4D Phantom 66-8734, flown by 1/Lt John Markle and Capt Stephen Eeaves, achieved a good lock-on and ripple-fired two Sparrows. Markle was treated to the remarkable sight of his missiles rushing out 15 degrees to starboard and slamming into the MiG-21 just behind its cockpit. His first missile blew the enemy aircraft in half. Remaining MiGs still coming head-on toward OYSTER flight salvoed their IR missiles blindly in a panicked reaction to Markle and Eaves joining the ranks of MiG killers—even though these missiles were useless in the frontal assault mode. Phantoms did not often get a 'clear shot' in a head-to-head confrontation but when they did, their Sparrow capability gave them absolute supremacy.

No one could have convinced Lodge's number 4. OYSTER 4, flown by 1/Lt Tommy Feezel and Capt Lawrence Pettit, was dead weight today. Several times on this day, OYSTER 4 would have clear, unimpeded opportunities to shoot at MiGs. But Feezel's radar had failed. With a point-blank battle suddenly raging all around him, smoke trails, sputtering missiles, fireballs and debris all about, Feezel could not track MiGs or guide missiles. Since he had no gun—fuel tanks had encumbered the Sidewinder pylons—the malfunction was to cost Feezel two certain MiG kills.

Bob Lodge threw OYSTER flight into a hard right 'break' as an onrushing MiG-21 narrowly missed a head-on collision. Suddenly, Lodge was right behind another MiG-21, but at 200 ft (60 m) he was much too close to use his missiles and, again, his F-4D had no gun. Lodge manoeuvred to gain separation to enable his missiles to arm and guide. The MiG climbed. Lodge followed.

Successful in shielding the assault on the Yen Bien rail yards and the Paul Doumer Bridge—not a single Air Force plane fell in either attack, and the MiGs never reached them—OYSTER flight

was now up to its ears in MiGs. As the fight unfolded, OYSTER 3, 66-7463 piloted by Capt Richard S 'Steve' Ritchie took advantage of the Phantom's sturdiness under heavy G forces to manoeuvre behind a MiG-21. Ritchie placed the 'dot' of his sight on the MiG and switched the fire-control system to auto-acquisition. His WSO, Capt Charles B DeBellevue, urged him to wait a few seconds to confirm a solid radar lock-on. Ritchie was at 18,000 ft (5,490 m) a mile behind and slightly below the MiG-21 which began a turn as he fired two SARH Sparrows. The first missile shot away, armed itself, bored at the target—and missed. The second hit the MiG right where its wing roots joined the fuselage and the Russian-made fighter came flying apart in a flashing explosion. The pilot got out somehow and his chute opened.

Later, Ritchie would rack up five kills to become the US Air Force's first ace. DeBellevue would get six MiGs to become the ranking figure among the five men to attain ace status in Vietnam. Another WSO, Capt Jeffrey Feinstein, would be the US Air Force's third ace. But today, these men were only beginning.

Today, the expertise of pitting the Phantom against the MiG, and the prospect of honours and recognition, seemed to be the province of OYSTER lead's Bob Lodge and Roger Locher. And with all of the early-warning aids available to Lodge, with RED CROWN and DISCO watching on radar, with BALTER and TAHOE flights nearby now, and with eight pairs of eyes in Oyster flight, *nobody* saw the four MiG-19s that popped out of cloud and latched onto Bob Lodge's tail.

By the time OYSTER 2 spotted them, it was too late. Markle shouted, 'OYSTER lead, you have MiGs at your ten o'clock!' Lodge was still closing behind a MiG-21 and may have believed he could kill the -21 before the MiG-19s could reach him. Or, in the confusion of battle, he may not have heard the warning. Markle looked on from close range but Phantom 65-784 did not waiver. The MiG-19s settled in 1,500 ft (460 m) behind Oyster lead and opened fire with their cannons.

Maj Lodge fired another Sparrow at the MiG-21. Again, Markle's voice: 'Hey, lead, break right! *Break right*!' They are *firing at you*!' To Markle, it looked as if the aggressive MiG-19s had joined formation with Bob Lodge's Phantom.

Markle watched Lodge's plane explode. Back-seater Roger Locher blew his canopy and ejected. OYSTER 3 and 4 would fight more MiGs on the way out of Vietnam. At one point, Lt Feezel would have a perfect Sparrow shot at a MiG-21— and no radar. Elsewhere in the Hanoi region, HARLOW 4 of the strike force escort, an F-4E Phantom 67-386 of the 334 TFS 432 TRW was shot down by MiG-19s. This, plus the loss of

OYSTER lead's Bob Lodge, a superb officer, darkened the spirits of men who'd downed three MiGs in a single battle, protected the strike force against heavy odds, and dealt a punishing blow to the North Vietnamese.

Alone and Unarmed

Don Pickard took his RF-4C in an abrupt climb to 43,000 ft (13,100 m), mindful that fuel is eaten more slowly at altitude. He needed a tanker now, badly. He had always been careful about conserving energy and watching the fuel flow, but this was one time when there seemed no solution to his problem. A hasty exchange of communication told him that there was no tanker in the right position offshore to top off his tanks. He idled back one engine, switched channels, and heard that the traffic pattern around Udorn was cluttered with aircraft returning with battle damage. He would have to set up a long, straight-in glide to Nam Phong, which was 40 miles (64 km) farther but had less traffic.

His backseater was now a helpless passenger as Pickard egressed and crossed Laos near Vientiane. He was now 100 miles (161 km) from home with 900 lb (408 kg) of fuel and the certain knowledge that FALCON 2 was burning 100 lb (45 kg) per minute. Worse, as has been noted earlier with respect to the F-4C model, the RF-4C fuel gauge was accurate only to within 200 lb (90 kg) at best. Said his WSO, 'What do you want me to do?' Said Pickard, who didn't like interruption of the radio traffic telling him about the situation at Udorn and Nam Phong, 'Shut up and pray!' The Phantom is not supposed to be flown on one engine, not ever, but the fuel situation was desperate. Pickard would be asked how far back he had set the idled engine. 'I had it set back to *off*. . .'

Cunningham and Driscoll

Cunningham and Driscoll's second MiG engagement came as they sighted a group of eight MiG-17s in a tight defensive wheel with three Phantoms swirling around inside the circle. The time was 1400. The Phantoms appeared to be in serious trouble. Later, the Navy would receive credit for instituting dissimilar air combat manoeuvre (ACM) training before the Air Force did and would be questioned for putting leading-edge manoeuvre slats on its Phantoms only long after the Air Force. These F-4J pilots had the advantage of the ACM training but not the slats. Cunningham turned to engage and as he did so one of the trapped Phantoms broke out of the wheel and almost collided with him. Another Phantom remained in serious trouble, under heavy fire. Both Cunningham and Driscoll identified it as SHOWTIME 112, the same plane (157267) they'd

flown in two earlier dogfights, now crewed by Cdr Dwight Timm and Lt Jim Fox. Timm was going around in a tight turn and had two MiG-17s in position on him, one approximately 2,000 ft (610 m) behind the other flying wing on the first MiG.

The MiG beside the one that was firing posed the real threat. Timm did not see it. In closing to engage against superior numbers, Cunningham would later be nominated for the Medal of Honor, although the medal was never awarded. As he closed, Cunningham also saw a MiG-21 close behind the two MiG-17s. Cunningham came down on the MiGs at their seven o'clock position bringing with him four more MiG-17s which had been out of range and now sensed a kill. Cunningham heard the growl of a good tone on his Sidewinder but was unable to determine if the missile was tracking the particular MiG which was close to shooting Timm down. Cunningham's hesitation is an important matter of historical record—evidence that getting a wingman out of trouble was more important to him than racking up kills. Cdr Timm was still unaware of the threat, believing that Cunningham's frantic warnings applied to others behind him. Amid this chaos, two MiG-19s joined the fight and curved down on Cunningham's tail.

By manoeuvring his Phantom with Driscoll keeping watch on the MiG-19s, Cunningham was able to keep the enemy fighters behind him at the six o'clock position—intentionally accepting risk—and this enabled him to keep the rest of the flight to his ten o'clock, giving him a better angle on the MiG-17 behing Timm. He was thinking and re-thinking everything that raged around him while four MiG-21s hung behind in the distance awaiting the outcome of the close-range duel. Cdr Timm broke away, leaving Cunningham with a clear field of fire at the MiG-17 in front of his Phantom. Cunningham fired the Sidewinder. It went up the MiG's tailpipe and blew it up. The pilot ejected. North Vietnamese pilot and ejection seat came spinning backward, narrowly missing Cunningham's aircraft.

As the MiG-17 went down, the MiG-21s rolled in.

Cdr Timm dived to lower altitude to gain some much-needed speed and bored away from the enemy threat. Cunningham—separated from his wingman—broke into the MiGs, causing them to overshoot and allowing him to break free. In his earphones, the carrier air wing commander, HONEYBEE, Cdr Gus Eggert, was calling for all of his fighters to disengage. The Navy strikes on the rail yard had now been completed successfully and fuel was becoming critical.

Cunningham began to depart the area unaware that the MiG-17 was gaining behind him. Lt Michael J Connelly and Lt Thomas J J Blonski in another VF-96 Phantom, 155769, coded NG-106, saw the intruder and shouted a warning. Cunningham applied full power. Connelly and Blonski in SHOWTIME 106 now had a chance to shoot. They had already downed one MiG and now their Sidewinders destroyed a second, probably saving Duke Cunningham's hide.

As he headed east toward the Gulf of Tonkin, Cunningham spotted yet another MiG-17 coming straight toward him. This MiG was piloted by the man who had seemed to outfight the Americans in 1965–68, outfight even the best of them—Robin Olds, Chappie James, Boots Blesse—and who was rated as North Vietnam's top fighter ace with credit for thirteen Phantoms. Col Tomb, alias Comrade Toon, had arrived.

Cunningham took evasive action. He pulled into a climb and the MiG went with him.

Much to his surprise, Cunningham was able to look out through his canopy and see the MiG pilot just before the North Vietnamese lost the advantage in the climb. As they went over the top of the climb pulling heavy G, the MiG slid in behind the Phantom and started shooting—but he had waited too long. Cunningham gained separation and re-engaged. Then, to his frustration because of its superior turning ability at medium altitude, the MiG-17 clawed behind him again.

Cunningham was again obliged to use the Phantom's superior acceleration to break off. On his third engagement with the tenacious enemy, he changed his tactics. As they went up into the climb again, he reduced power and extended his speed brakes momentarily. It was a risky manoeuvre but, as he'd hoped, the MiG overshot. As they went over the top again, Cunningham managed to stay behind the MiG who suddenly broke off the engagement and dived away. Despite the probability of its IR seeker being confused by heat returns from the ground and in an awkward look-down attitude, Cunningham fired a Sidewinder. It guided correctly and exploded close enough to the MiG to cause it to crash without recovering from its dive. Now getting desperately low on fuel and with numerous MiGs still in the area, Cunningham again turned for the coast, the thought not yet firmly fixed in his mind that he and Driscoll had just become aces.

OYSTER Flight

When he bailed out of Bob Lodge's F-4D, Capt Roger C Locher was at the end of his 407th combat mission as a WSO in F-4s. Later in his career, Locher would become a front-seat pilot and fly F-4Es with the 43rd Tactical Fighter Squadron in Alaska—as would OYSTER 3's DeBellevue—but on 10 May 1972, Locher had little reason to believe that he would live much longer than Lodge had.

Locher survived the ejection and descent and landed in a forest some ninety miles inside North Vietnam. No man had ever been rescued this deep in enemy territory.

Roger Locher remained on the ground and evaded capture by North Vietnamese troopers for an unprecedented *twenty-three days*! He was eventually recovered in the most daring and farthest-north rescue of the war. The operation was conducted in close proximity to a MiG airbase and involved some thirty-eight US aircraft and helicopters. It was by far the longest any American survived in North Vietnam without being captured.

Cunningham and Driscoll

For SHOWTIME 100, this long day was still not over. Cunningham had a welcome view of the sea and was climbing for the coast to conserve fuel. Missile warnings were being broadcast in his earphones, but Cunningham was intent on the fuel situation. Neither he nor Driscoll saw the SAM rushing up at them until too late.

Hai Duong Bridge: Mike Ruth

Air-to-air combat may be a joust between warriors but it must never be forgotten that Phantoms fought MiGs for the central purpose of freeing strike aircraft to assault North Vietnamese targets. Mike Ruth knew it when he woke up that morning. 'You're sober and silent before a mission. You'll talk wildly when it's over but beforehand you're scared, just plain scared, and you don't want yourself to know it.' Typical of strike missions on 10 May was the 37-plane A-6 and A-7 attack from Lt Ruth's ship *Kitty Hawk* (CVA-63), flown against the 'other' bridge, the strategic railroad and highway span at Hai Duong.

Although less well known than the Paul Doumer Bridge (or the Thanh Hoa, a classic Phantom target outside the scope of this work), the Hai Duong Bridge—associated with the rail yards of the same name attacked earlier in the day—was a vital link between Hanoi and Haiphong. As official Navy orders describe it, 'The destruction of this vital bridge would cut the east-west flow of military supplies and limit the enemy's freedom of logistical movement in support of their (sic) forces in the south.'

Top cover for *Kitty Hawk*'s strike force came

The point of Phantoms fighting MiGs was to permit the attack force to bring North Vietnam to a settlement. On 10 May 1972, Lt Michael A Ruth of the 'Dambusters' of VA-195 from Kitty Hawk pulls off the Hai Duong Bridge in A-7E Corsair 157526, callsign CHIPPIE 403. The effect of Mike's 1,000-lb and 2,000-lb bombs on the bridge span is apparent in this photo taken by the KV-72 camera aboard wingman Lt Charlie Brewer's A-7E Corsair
(US Navy)

from Phantoms of the 'Aardvarks' of VF-114,
callsign LINFIELD, and the 'Black Lions' of VF-
213, callsign BLACKBURN. Both squadrons
would score MiG kills during this campaign, but
not on this day—although they tangled furiously
with Tomb's pilots.

Against the bridge itself flew A-6A Intruders of
the 'Knight Riders' of VA-52, callsign VICEROY,
and A-7E Corsairs of the 'Golden Dragons' of
VA-192, callsign JURY and the 'Dambusters' of
VA-195, callsign CHIPPIE. The Dambusters had
earned their name taking out Yalu River
hydroelectric dams during the 1950–3 Korean
War, but this was a tougher job. Fifteen SAM
sites were clustered immediately around the Hai
Duong Bridge. To counter them came VA-195's
executive officer, Lt Cdr Norman D Campbell,
whose first impression of the Phantom appears on
page 36 and who, today, was flying A-7E Corsair
156858, callsign CHIPPIE 405, with four AGM-

45 Shrike missiles. Campbell's Iron Hand or SAM
suppression mission was timed to cover the ingress
and egress of the strike force. Campbell and his
wingmen were under constant AAA fire from the
coast in, with SAMs being launched at them
repeatedly.

To attack the bridge's centre span came, among
others, VA-195's Lt Charlie Brewer and Lt
Michael A Ruth. Mike Ruth was at the controls of
A-7E Corsair 157526, callsign CHIPPIE 403. Due
to the long ingress and egress, the strike aircraft
were each loaded with two Mk 83 1,000-lb (454-
kg) and Mk 84 2,000-lb (908-kg) bombs on parent
racks which combined minimal drag with heavy
punch. Though the bridge had been assaulted by
an earlier wave of strike aircraft, Mike Ruth could
see that it was still standing as he began his run-
in. SAMs were flying everywhere. Tracers
crisscrossed the air in front of him. Ruth does not
remember if he was thinking about MiGs at the

time but part of his thinking was instinctive: 'You knew the Phantoms were up there to keep MiGs off your back. You had confidence they would do it.'

Ruth's citation for the Distinguished Service Cross says that he 'continually maintained close section integrity . . . despite intense enemy opposition. Positioning his aircraft at an optimum roll-in point, Lt Ruth commenced a devastating attack and despite a wall of intensive anti-aircraft artillery fire placed all ordnance directly on target.' Ruth acknowledges that this is very dry language for the feeling in his gut as he pulled CHIPPIE 403 off the target behind Brewer, banked, and saw their bombs rip the huge bridge to pieces.

Cunningham and Driscoll

SHOWTIME 100 shook violently as the missile exploded beneath it. For a moment, Cunningham

thought he'd been spared by a 'near miss' as the F-4J Phantom continued climbing. Then, hydraulic gauges started to fluctuate. Flames, fed by fuel escaping from punctured fuel cells, spewed back in the airplane's wake. As the needles dropped to zero, the aircraft started to pitch up. Fighting now with his only control left, Cunningham rolled the Phantom by using manual rudder. Each time the nose pitched above the horizon, he used his strength on the rudder to force the nose back down, and as it started down he used opposite afterburner to keep the nose from getting dangerously low. In what may have been his most extraordinary flying feat of the day, Cunningham kept the Phantom in the air long enough to get across the coastline.

155800 was now sending back a gushing stream of flame and smoke. The fire burned through the remaining controls and the F-4J went into a spin. They were tumbling below the 10,000 ft (3,050 m) mark now and Cunningham told his RIO the obvious. 'We have to get out.'

Cunningham and Driscoll ejected. For a terrifying moment, it seemed the wind would carry their chutes back into North Vietnam. But they hit the water offshore while the Phantom plunged to its destruction. Shore guns began firing in the hope of hitting the two Navy fliers but a Marine HH-46A Sea Knight helicopter from the USS *Okinawa* (LPH-11) snatched them from the churning sea and carried them to the deck of the destroyer tender USS *Samuel Gompers* (AD-37). In a short time, the first Phantom aces were again safely aboard *Constellation*. Ironically, theirs was the only aircraft lost by VF-96 during this cruise.

Alone and Unarmed

Many men were returning from the Phantom's longest day with battle damage, fuel starvation, and a myriad of problems caused by flying steel and broken pieces. The fact that enemy action had claimed only four Phantoms in the biggest battle yet fought was tribute to the toughness of the aircraft. But, still, the men limped home, to *Constellation*, to *Coral Sea*, to Udorn, to Ubon, diversions to Da Nang.

Few had as many problems as Don Pickard who was forced to coax every last drop of fuel in the starving engine he *hadn't* idled back to off. Don was still in formation with FALCON lead, Maj Rogers, but you could never be certain and for all he knew he might have the *only* pictures to permit

The victors. The first American air aces in two decades, Lt Randall Cunningham and Lt (jg) William P Driscoll return to Constellation *(CVA-64) after the day they shot down three MiGs, took out North Vietnam's key fighter wing commander, and were shot down by an SA-2 surface-to-air missile. Their F-4J Phantom (155800) lies at the bottom of the Gulf of Tonkin (US Navy)*

Living again his air battle with North Vietnam's MiG-17 fighter ace Col Tomb, Commander Randy Cunningham flies with his hands at Falcon Field, Mesa, Arizona in January 1984. The MiG-17 was donated to the American Fighter Aces Museum by King Hassan of Morocco whose air force flew Soviet equipment in the 1950s (Douglas E Slowiak)

TOP LEFT
Surrounded by 'Fighting Falcons' of VF-96, Lt Randall Cunningham is below decks aboard Constellation *(CVA-64) using his hands to describe to fellow F-4J Phantom pilots the killing of Colonel Tomb (US Navy)*

OPPOSITE
Lt Randall Cunningham (left) and Lt (jg) William P Driscoll—'Duke' and 'Irish' in the nicknames all naval aviators acquire—recover from the air battle over North Vietnam which made them aces (US Navy)

intelligence analysts to size up the Air Force strikes on Yen Bien and the Paul Doumer Bridge. (This turned out to be true; FALCON lead suffered a camera failure). Don's earphones told him again and again of chaos and confusion at his home base, Udorn, where he kept hearing talk of 'coming home with battle damage.' Nam Phong remained his best hope.

He was still at 16,000 ft (4,880 m), as high as possible on approach to save fuel, when Nam Phong cleared him for a straight-in approach. It was time to re-start the idle engine. The moment Capt Pickard did so, the cockpit de-fog system filled the inside of his canopy with ice!

He'd had a quick distant glimpse at runway's end far ahead, then limited vision, then none. Nam Phong was nicknamed the 'Rose Garden'—the US Marine Phantom squadron there, the 'Red Devils' of VMFA-232, flying F-4Js, would be the last Americans to leave Southeast Asia in September 1973—but the name was macabre American humour. It was a flat dry place with choking red dust everywhere, known for strong crosswinds, not an easy place to land at the best of times—and now Capt Pickard couldn't even see it! And Don's fuel reading was already below the full amount of its margin of error.

The ice packed up inside his windshield. As he dropped half flaps and lowered the gear, the RF-4C seemed to protest. Rogers' voice confirmed the gear down, but for a brief moment Don wasn't sure where Rogers was. There would be only one chance. There was no fuel for a go-around. Sid Rogers moved closer to talk him in.

Pilots say the Phantom is an easy, well-handling ship on a controlled GCA approach. In a serious situation, indeed an emergency, pilots think instead of the Phantom's trickiness at flareout and touchdown. Pickard hit the ground in a good solid landing and turned off the taxiway with just 200 lb (90 kg) of fuel left in his tanks, barely enough to

Over the Sea of Japan where North Korean fighters shot down a US Navy EC-121 Constellation three months earlier, F-4J Phantom (153809) of the 'Black Knights' of VF-154 from Ranger *(CVA-61) guards against any further adventurism by Pyongyang in January 1970 (US Navy)*

OPPOSITE PAGE
Capt Jeff Feinstein of the 555th Tactical Fighter Squadron, a back-seat weapons systems officer, became an air ace during the Linebacker campaign by shooting down five MiGs (US Air Force)

park. His had been a long day and he had won the Distinguished Service Cross.

May 10, 1972 was *the* day in combat for the Phantom. Recce pictures brought back by Capt Pickard confirmed that the air-to-air fighting, by keeping the MiGs away from the strike force, had enabled the air-to-ground combatants to inflict devastating blows on North Vietnam. The Air Force F-4s carrying 500-lb (227-kg) conventional bombs had isolated the Yen Bien marshalling yard by cratering both entrances to the complex. Navy strike aircraft, including F-4Js, had done a similar job on Haiphong POL facilities and the Hai Duong rail yard. At the Paul Doumer Bridge, twenty-two laser-guided and seven electro-optically guided 2,000-lb (908-kg) bombs had been dropped. Twelve had achieved direct hits, four had probably done so, and the remainder had had unconfirmed results.

The combined Air Force/Navy operations over North Vietnam had produced eleven MiG kills with four Phantom losses, although the MiGCAP Phantoms had been tasked primarily with 'protecting the force' rather than bagging enemy

fighters. If legend is to be believed, Duke Cunningham had killed North Vietnam's key fighter wing commander, although it was small recompense for the loss of good men like Maj Bob Lodge.

The rematch, the second campaign against North Vietnam, would continue. There would be more F-4 Phantom achievements, more MiG victories, more losses. The 'in country war' in South Vietnam would continue too, where Air Force, Navy and Marine Phantom crews would wage their seemingly endless war against ground targets. The Marines, in particular, warrant more space than this volume contains. On 11 September 1972, Maj Lee T 'Bear' Lasseter and Capt John D Cummings, in an F-4J Phantom 155526 of the 'Shamrocks' of VMFA-333 would become the only Marine crew to score an air-to-air kill in a Marine aircraft—shooting down a MiG-21 with a Sidewinder—although, like Cunningham and Driscoll, they would end their big mission with their feet wet.

Following a brief lull to grease negotiations in November, the Linebacker campaign would be

May 1972 MiG killer. Four days before the air battles in this chapter, McAir ship 242, an F-4B-13-MC Phantom 150456, of squadron VF-51, callsign SCREAMING EAGLE 100, shot down a MiG-17 at the hands of Lt Cdr Jerry B Houston and Lt Kevin T Moore. Shown here on 11 June 1978 with the 'Hell's Angels' of Marine reserve squadron VMFA-321 at Andrews AFB, Maryland after being converted to F-4N-18-MC, aircraft 150456 wears a 'MiG kill' star on its splitter vane. In 1984, it was still in service with VMFA-321 but in 'low visibility' camouflage with the MiG kill removed
(US Marine Corps)

OPPOSITE PAGE
Over the Gulf of Tonkin on a Rolling Thunder mission in March 1968, F-4B Phantom (152996) of the 'Black Lions' of VF-213 takes on fuel from a KA-3B Skywarrior tanker
(US Navy)

replaced by Linebacker II, the massive Christmas bombing which broke the enemy's warfighting potential and produced a settlement. The last MiG kill of the war came on 12 January 1973 when Lt Victor T Kovaleski and Lt (jg) James A Wise, flying from *Midway* (CVA-41) in an F-4B Phantom 153045, coded NG-102, callsign ROCK RIVER 102, downed a MiG-17 with a Sidewinder. Thus, the F-4B model and the *Midway* scored the first and last kills of the war, nearly eight years apart. The final box score for air-to-air combat over North Vietnam was 193 enemy aircraft shot down vis-a-vis 92 American aircraft lost. It was better than Rolling Thunder. It was not good enough. But the two to one kill ratio was misleading. Americans had travelled far into North Vietnam to fight, refuelling aloft for the first time in any war, carrying their fuel and ordnance deep into the homeland of an enemy who had had to do none of these things. The Phantom had won the rematch.

American forces withdrew. Prisoners of war came home on 4 March 1973—for Maj Kenneth W Cordier, after six years and four months as a prisoner. When the negotiated settlement did not hold and it all came to an end on 30 April 1975, American forces returned briefly for Operation Frequent Wind—the evacuation of Saigon—and *Midway*'s Phantoms were joined in the sad task of covering the withdrawal by the fighter which would replace them on carrier decks, the Grumman F-14 Tomcat.

Table 5-1. The MiG killers of May 10th, 1972

Aircraft	Serial	Tailcode	Callsign	Unit	Crew	Kill
F-4D	65-784	OY	OYSTER 1	555 TFS 432 TRW	Maj Robert N Lodge / Capt Roger C Locher	MiG-21
F-4D	66-7463	OY	OYSTER 3	555 TFS 432 TRW	Capt Richard S Ritchie / Capt Charles B DeBellevue	MiG-21
F-4D	66-8734	OY	OYSTER 2	555 TFS 432 TRW	1/Lt John D Markle / Capt Stephen D Eaves	MiG-21
Constellation (CVA-64):						
F-4J	157269	NG-211	SILVER KITE 211	VF-92 CVW-9	Lt Curt Dose / Lt Cdr James McDevitt	MiG-21F
F-4J	155769	NG-106	SHOWTIME 106	VF-96 CVW-9	Lt Michael J Connelly / Lt Thomas J J Blonski	MiG-17
F-4J	155769	NG-106	SHOWTIME 106	VF-96 CVW-9	Lt Michael J Connelly / Lt Thomas J J Blonski	MiG-17
F-4J	155749	NG-111	SHOWTIME 111	VF-96 CVW-9	Lt Steven C Shoemaker / Lt (jg) Keith V Crenshaw	MiG-17
F-4J	155800	NG-100	SHOWTIME 100	VF-96 CVW-9	Lt Randall H Cunningham / Lt (jg) William P Driscoll	MiG-17
F-4J	155800	NG-100	SHOWTIME 100	VF-96 CVW-9	Lt Randall H Cunningham / Lt (jg) William P Driscoll	MiG-17
F-4J	155800	NG-100	SHOWTIME 100	VF-96 CVW-9	Lt Randall H Cunningham / Lt (jg) William P Driscoll	MiG-17
Coral Sea (CVA-43):						
F-4B	151398	NL-110	SCREAMING EAGLE 111	VF-51 CVW-11	Lt Kenneth L Cannon / Lt Roy A Morris, Jr	MiG-17

Chapter 6
Israel
The Phantom Under the Star of David

Following the Six Day War of 1967 and Israel's dramatic trouncing of its Arab neighbours, the United States 'refusal' to sell F-4 Phantoms to Jerusalem was a sorely contested issue in Washington, especially on Capitol Hill.

The Israeli Defence Force/Air Force (IDF/AF), or *Tsvah Haganah Le Israel/Heyl Ha'Avir* was urgently in need of a first-line aircraft for the ground attack role. The IDF/AF was equipped principally with the Sud-Ouest Vautour of 1950s vintage plus about 65 supersonic French-built Mirage IIIs, some of which had been lost in the Six Day War and were not likely to be replaced. Egypt, in contrast, remained heavily armed with about 100 MiG-21s and 60 Sukhoi fighters.

In January 1968, the US completed delivery of 48 A-4 Skyhawks which had been promised before the war and President Johnson promised Premier Eshkol about 20 additional A-4s. But the A-4, despite its longevity and stretching potential, was not a first-line aircraft either, and in March 1968 France reaffirmed its ban on delivery of 50 Mirage fighter-bombers pending 'serious' talks to ease

tensions in the Middle East. The view from Jerusalem must have seemed especially grim when the French agreed to supply Mirages to Iraq but not to Israel. Although President Johnson tended to oppose the sale of Phantoms and *The New York Times* opined that the sale would accelerate an arms race with the Arabs, domestic pressure was building on the White House from American citizens and congressmen who feared that the 'refusal' would jeopardize Israel's security.

In the end, after candidate Richard M Nixon announced that he favoured the deal, on 9 October 1968 Johnson began negotiations with Jerusalem for the sale of Phantoms. When Nixon was elected in November, the sale became inevitable. The announcement was made on 27 December of the sale of 50 F-4 Phantoms to Israel, to be delivered

Early Phantom for Israel. One of the first machines built for the Israeli Defence Force/Air Force was F-4E-39-MC Phantom 68-436, McAir ship 3567, shown with Israeli camouflage but US-style markings at the builder's St Louis facility in August 1969. Records show that this aircraft has subsequently been attrited (MDC)

late in 1969 at a cost of more than $200 million
(£81 million)—at the time, the largest arms
transaction between the two countries. It was
reported that Israel had ordered 'one of the most
expensive models of the F-4, equipped with bomb
racks,' although all Phantoms had bomb racks and
it later became evident that these were standard
fiscal year 1968 F-4Es then coming into
widespread service. These machines, commencing
with airframe 68-396, had the internal nose
M61A1 Vulcan 20-mm cannon but did not have
the leading-edge manoeuvre slats, TISEO, or
'ergonometric' cockpit layout of later F-4Es. At
least ten Phantoms and possibly a squadron of 16
would be delivered in late 1969 and the bulk in
1970. At that juncture in history, 50 Phantoms was
regarded as an enormous force and it was not
envisaged that total Israeli F-4E strength would
one day reach 204.

The War of Attrition

Though the 1967 war was over, the IDF/AF was
almost immediately plunged into a new conflict,
the War of Attrition—from Jerusalem's viewpoint,
a struggle for survival against terrorists. At the end
of 1967, Israeli planes bombed terrorist
concentrations in Jordan and silenced Jordanian
artillery which had been shelling the Jordan Valley
settlements. IDF/AF helicopters pursued intruders
who had penetrated Israeli territory, enabling
ground forces to find and destroy them.

The introduction of Phantoms was especially
important because of the French embargo on
further Mirages. In March 1969, 120 selected
fliers, mostly former Mirage pilots, arrived at
George AFB, California with technicians and
ground crews to begin training. Meanwhile, the
War of Attrition was coalescing as a struggle in
which airpower would be needed to compensate
for Israeli inferiority in artillery along the Suez
Canal.

The first Phantoms arrived after a long ferry
flight in September 1969 and a host of Israeli
leaders welcomed the arrival of a machine they
expected would revolutionize their tactics. The F-
4Es were committed to combat on 7 January 1970
led by Sqn Ldr Samuel Chetz, already an ace,
against Soviet-constructed SAM and radar
installations at Dahashur. Chetz, known for his
aggressive spirit, was later killed in a low-level
strike on a SAM site—his loss enabling Jerusalem
to reveal his name while the identities of active
pilots remained undisclosed.

To redress the 'artillery gap,' Skyhawks and
Phantoms attacked and silenced Egyptian missile,
anti-aircraft, and artillery batteries. Soon,
Phantoms were making raids deep into Egyptian
territory. In one resourceful operation, the intrepid
Israelis heisted an entire Soviet radar station and

transported it back to Israel! By late January 1970,
the IDF/AF was regularly flying bombing
missions into the heart of Egypt.

The effectiveness of the Phantom clearly shook
Egyptian leaders, who watched their air defence
network being systematically destroyed in low-
level strikes by some F-4Es while others ranged
against targets deep in their territory. Soviet
personnel in Egypt became directly involved,
introducing the mobile SA-3 Goa surface-to-air
missile and piloting MiG-21J interceptors. Even
with their intervention, in the spring of 1970 the
IDF/AF commanded the initiative and F-4E
pilots—who had the traditional armament of AIM-
7 Sparrows and AIM-9 Sidewinders in addition to
the 20 mm cannon—were downing MiGs
regularly. On 30 July 1970, Soviet pilots tangled
with Israeli Phantoms in a raging dogfight over the
Gulf of Suez—the first time the Phantom's
internal cannon was fully tested in a major battle,
having not yet been unleashed in the skies of
North Vietnam—and the Israelis shot down five
MiG-21Js with no losses. Soon thereafter, on a
marathon 2,000-mile (3,220-km) strike mission to
Ras Banas, Phantoms bombed and sank a Komar-
class missile patrol boat and a 2,500-ton Z-class
destroyer.

Ultimately, the effectiveness of the Phantoms
and the aggressive prosecution of the war by Israel
was blunted by the expansion throughout Egypt of
a costly and extensive, Soviet-supported SAM
missile defence system. Considered by many a
'stand-off' between the F-4E Phantom and the
SA-2 Guideline surface-to-air missile (the SAM so
familiar to US airmen in Vietnam), the War of
Attrition was concluded with the cease-fire
agreement of 7 August 1970. In its last stages, the
principal problem facing IDF/AF pilots was
missile batteries supplied to the Egyptian and
Syrian armies, and the Israelis began to look for
the technological means to combat the enemy's
new weapons.

Israel and the Phantom

To a nation fiercely proud of its plucky and
undaunted air arm, the $4 million (£1.38 million)
per F-4E Phantom seemed a wise and prudent
purchase. Jerusalem went a step further, ordering
the RF-4E export reconnaissance variant, and at
one point borrowed from the US Air Force's 1st
Tactical Reconnaissance Squadron at Alconbury,
England a sole RF-4C airframe (69-370), which
appeared in desert camouflage in March 1971.
Eventually, Israel would have 12 RF-4Es, not
quite enough for its seven fighter squadrons to be
augmented with the traditional two machines each,
and at least one RF-4E would be noted with field
modification to carry Sidewinders. Once the flow
of Phantom deliveries began, US military

reservists under contract to McDonnell Douglas ferried the newly built aircraft from St Louis to the Azores, thence eastward with a stopover in Cyprus.

Official records credit Israeli F-4E Phantoms with 93 air-to-air victories of the 280 chalked up by the Phantom worldwide (as of 31 March 1984). It is not clear whether this figure includes the only shootdown of a Boeing 727 airliner—the most controversial 'kill' ever scored by Phantoms. In February 1973, Israeli F-4Es intercepted the Libyan jetliner when it penetrated Israeli-occupied Sinai Desert. The course of the Boeing seemed to suggest hostile intent—perhaps an intelligence-gathering mission. 'We tried desperately to force it down, not shoot it down,' said Maj General Mordechai Hud, IDF/AF chief. Two Phantom pilots exchanged hand signals with the Libyan pilot but were unable to persuade him to follow them to Bir Gafgafa Air Base. A Phantom fired a warning burst of 20-mm. The airliner lowered its wheels but then raised them again and banked in an apparent attempt to escape. The Phantoms shot it down. 105 of the 112 people aboard died.

A real war never seemed far away. Even before Phantoms began gaining an upper hand against MiGs in their second campaign over North Vietnam—the Linebacker operations from May 1972 to January 1973 which introduced 'smart' bombs, compartmentalized squadron mission assignments, and other innovations—*Air Enthusiast* magazine reported in 1971 that Israel was 'preparing for the second round.' Though the Soviet role in the Mideast confrontation was dramatically altered when President Sadat booted out Russian advisors on 18 July 1972, a formidable arsenal remained in the hands of Israel's Arab adversaries and there remained a strong sense that a new fight was impending. Like the Americans who had needed a rematch in North Vietnam to prevail over the MiG-17, MiG-19 and MiG-21, IDF/AF airmen believed that the decisive fight with Egyptian and Syrian airpower remained ahead. On 13 March 1973, US State Department officials reported that, in addition to further F-4E Phantoms already committed, Washington would sell Israel four squadrons of fighter-bombers—a mix of A-4 Skyhawks and improved F-4Es with slats, TISEO, and 'man efficient' cockpits—to be delivered by January 1974. So far, the Northrop television electro-optical guidance device, fitted in a cylindrical extension from the Phantom's port wing—was untested in air-to-air battle although the same principle—use of zoom-lens TV to guide ordnance—had planted bombs squarely in the centre of Hanoi's Doumer Bridge. The innovative Israelis had introduced new filips of their own, including extended muzzle housings to enhance the accuracy of the Vulcan 20-mm cannon. The new deliveries would greatly enhance Jerusalem's

military muscle and thereby aid efforts toward a peace settlement—but January 1974, it would turn out, would be too late. With stunning swiftness, the region erupted into conflict on the eve of the traditional Hebrew rite of atonement—6 October 1973, with a dramatic assault by Egyptian, Syrian and other Arab forces.

The Yom Kippur War

An official release states that 150 Phantoms made up the fighting spearhead of the IDF/AF as the Arabs' surprise attack was unleashed. In the early hours of the fighting, Egyptian Tupolev Tu-16 bombers carrying AS-5 air-to-surface standoff missiles pressed their attacks deep into Israeli territory. One Tu-16 was approaching Tel Aviv on the first day of the war, 6 October when shot down by an Israeli F-4E Phantom. While the full story of the war, like any full account of American fighting in Vietnam, lies beyond the scope of this work, it is apparent that Phantoms were quickly thrown into action on both major fronts and that they faced a variety of new threats, including vehicle-mounted SA-6 and shoulder-mounted SA-7 Strella surface-to-air misisiles. The Israelis struck decisively against Syrian SAM sites on October 7th and acknowledged the loss of one Phantom in that fighting. On the Syrian front, MiG-17s and Sukhois flew ground attack missions dscorted by MiG-21s and Iraqi Hunters. Israel struck back on October 9th by sending Phantoms to bomb downtown Damascus. Seeking to neutralize the Arabs' second front by securing the Golan Heights and blunting Syria's fighting potential, Israel confirmed yet another Phantom loss on October 11th. As the war intensified with constant air fighting 12–24 October, no further losses were publicly announced although both sides claimed to have destroyed large numbers of the other's aircraft.

No full account of the air fighting has been published by either side, and details of air-to-air kills remain sketchy. The Phantom appears to have been used primarily in the long-range strike role, with the Mirage III flying top cover, and most air-to-air engagements appear to have been fought mainly with IR-seeking air-to-air missiles, rarely at close enough distance to use guns. When they found themselves in close-quarters fights with very manoeuvrable MiGs and less effective Sukhois, Israeli pilots made use of notions about power and energy manoeuvrability devised by Maj John Boyd of the US Air Force's Prototype Study Group. Boyd's emphasis on the importance of specific excess power, the standard of thrust-to-weight ratio reached at various conditions of speed, altitude and manoeuvre, had arrived too late for the Linebacker campaign in North Vietnam and—to some fighter veterans—seemed an impertinence.

Israeli RF-4E. Painted in the desert camouflage scheme of the Israeli Defence Force/Air Force but temporarily wearing US national insignia, export reconnaissance RF-4E Phantom 69-7593 on a test flight at McDonnell's facility at Lambert Field in St Louis, on 8 April 1971 (Frederick W Roos)

Boyd was saying that the relationship between drag and thrust was what mattered in a close encounter. Since energy is lost climbing, increasing speed, or banking, a point can be reached where drag exceeds thrust and the pilot is then at the mercy of aerodynamic forces rather than in control of his aircraft. By paying judicious attention to the airplane's attitude and through

prudent use of afterburner—fuel depletion being less a problem in the Middle East fighting than in extended operations over North Vietnam—a well-trained pilot could seize and hold the initiative over his adversary. In certain manoeuvre situations, the level flight .73 to 1 thrust-to-weight ratio of the F-4E Phantom could be increased to a more advantageous .9 to 1 or better and by careful attention to energy manoeuvrability the F-4E could prevail over the MiG-21 even in a very close, protracted fight. Pilot experience was crucial, and IDF/AF fliers, although many seemed remarkably young, had an enormous advantage in experience. For some reason, the Israelis had never adopted the thinking of Capt Frank W Ault,

the US Navy officer who'd analyzed the
disappointing American showing during the
Rolling Thunder campaign and brought about the
creation of training in dissimilar air combat
manoeuvring (ACM), the US Navy's 'Top Gun'
effort at NAS Miramar, California and the US Air
Force's 'Red Flag' program at Nellis AFB,
Nevada.

Just as Americans in Vietnam found themselves
pitted against highly motivated, Soviet trained
pilots of great ability, the Israelis faced Egyptian
and Syrian fliers whose talent and aggressiveness
warrant mention. A fierce fighting spirit was
displayed by MiG pilots who seemed to be
directed by ground control to attack Israeli

Phantoms only when conditions of altitude,
possible surprise, and relative fuel advantage
favoured them. On occasion, a brace of MiG-21s
above a Phantom formation might make a single
diving, slashing attack—using the same calculation
and prudence exhibited by the North Vietnamese
and for the same purpose, namely to 'catch'
ordnance-laden F-4Es at disadvantage. While
attacking slower aircraft such as Skyhawks, the
MiGs often made the mistake of slowing down
while achieving missile lock-on, giving the
IDF/AF pilot room to out-turn them.

Although IDF/AF losses in the October 1973
war may seem small in abolute numbers, most
occurred in the early period of fighting and, when

Tail of Israeli F-4E, May 1980. Note the innovative
censorship on the rudder—why bother to censor the
photograph when you can use sticky tape on the aircraft?

OPPOSITE
F-4E Phantom of the Israeli Air Force/Defense Force on
display with typical ordnance in May 1980
(MDC)

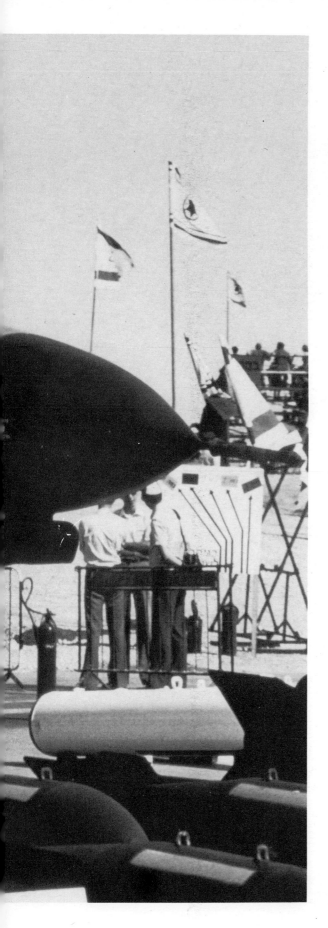

forty-five A-4 Skyhawk losses are included,
represented a full 20 per cent of the warplanes
Israel had received from the US. Before the war,
the US had been delivering Phantoms at the rate
of two per month. Premier Meier's government
immediately asked for more aircraft, more quickly.
Though plans had originally called for all Israeli
F-4Es to come from new production in St Louis,
as part of a massive supply and support effort the
US agreed to deliver F-4Es from its own
inventory, with Jerusalem later to purchase
'payback' airframes for US use. Operation Nickel
Grass was mounted, US Air Force F-4Es being
ferried direct to Tel Aviv and immediately thrown
into battle once modified with the Israeli-style
probe refuelling receptacle on the right front
fuselage in place of the US Air Force dorsal
receptacle. One Nickel Grass, TISEO-equipped
late-model F-4E actually went into battle still
wearing an SJ tailcode signifying that it had just
arrived from Col Len C Russell's 4th Tactical
Fighter Wing at Seymour Johnson AFB, North
Carolina. 32 members of the 4 TFW received
awards from Tactical Air Command chief Gen
Robert J Dixon for their 12–15 October
participation in Operation Peace Echo, the wing's
portion of the Nickel Grass effort. Other F-4Es

An Israeli F-4E Phantom being used as a testbed, with two Gabriel Mk 3 anti-shipping missiles, one under each wing, tucks in its wheels on take-off (IAI)

BELOW
Israeli F-4E with Gabriel anti-shipping missiles (IAI)

reportedly were delivered from the US Air Force's 401st Tactical Fighter Wing at Torrejon AB Spain, and that wing's 614th Tactical Fighter Squadron abruptly converted from the F-4E variant to the F-4D (not used by Israel) shortly after October 1973. Thirty-four F-4Es were diverted to Israel as a result of the Nickel Grass undertaking.

It was to be a source of immense pride that, in a tough and bitter war which proved the fighting mettle of their Arab opponents, Israel would lose *not a single Phantom* in air-to-air combat, although Jerusalem would acknowledge 22 Phantom losses to SAM and AAA fire. One of these F-4E Phantoms, 69-7248, would turn up later in pieces in a Cairo Museum.

The Yom Kippur War, in which the F-4 Phantom seems to have acquitted itself well, was also the impetus for steps which would push the Phantom into the background as Israel sought more advanced first-line fighter aircraft. By 1975, the debate was over the advanced F-15 Eagle, with the Defence Department announcing that Jerusalem would have to 'stand in line' for the new fighter under the presidential arms-transfer policy then in effect and Congressman Robert L Leggett, Jr, among others, arguing that the sale of the F-15 was unnecessary. Stung by its dependence on outside help during the conflict, Israel's leaders also moved to become more self-sufficient, unveiling the locally-developed Kfir

fighter on 15 April 1975 and announcing the more advanced, indigenous Lavi fighter project on 1 March 1980. In September 1979, in Operation Peace Pharaoh, thirty-five F-4E Phantoms with high airframe hours were supplied to Egypt from US Air Force inventory in a move seen by many as a 'balancing' gesture at a time when relations between Egypt and Israel had improved, although the expense and complexity of maintaining the Phantom seems to have hindered its effectiveness in Egyptian service and Cairo has since acquired F-16s. The Peace Pharaoh aircraft came from Col William A Gorton's 31st Tactical Fighter Wing at Homestead AFB, Florida.

By the mid-1980s, the F-15 And F-16 were the principal fighters in Israeli service and the Phantom may have won mention in its final combat action in September 1979 when F-15 Eagles shot down four Syrian MiGs attempting to prevent an RF-4E Phantom from carrying out reconnaissance duties. Israel's announcement that a MiG-25 Foxbat was shot down by an F-15 on 13 February 1981 is the best hint yet that *all* IDF/AF Phantoms may one day find themselves relics in museums! Still, the Phantom soldiers on today—having proven an effective testbed for the Gabriel Mk 3 anti-shipping 'fire and forget' missile and retaining a role in the IDF/AF fighter force. Museum curators would be advised to wait a time longer before expecting Israeli Phantoms to be categorized as surplus.

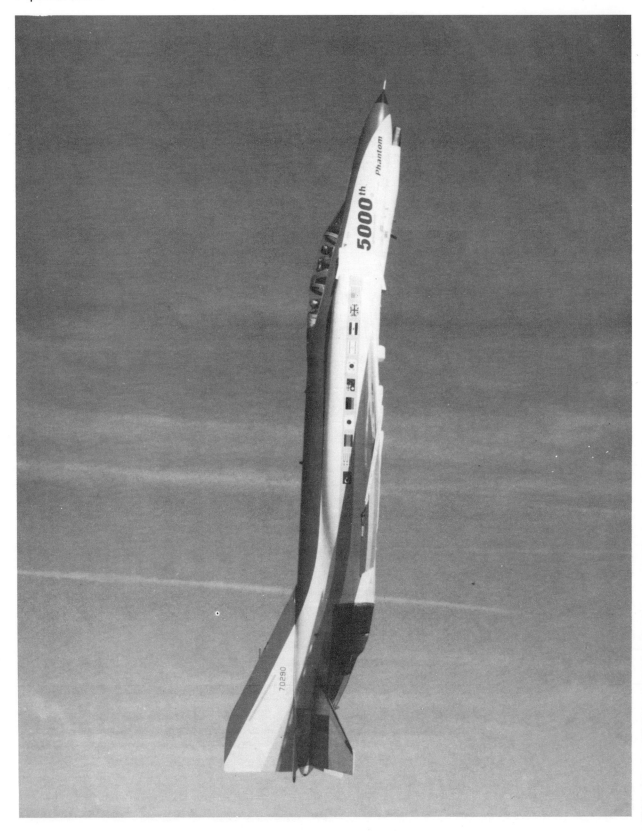

Going up . . . the five thousandth machine, F-4E-65-MC
Phantom 77-290 pictured in March 1978. This example is
currently in service with the Turkish Air Force
(MDC)

Chapter 7
Overseas Phantoms
The Phantom in Foreign Colours

All morning, the howl of Phantoms had echoed in the city of Seoul. At 11:48 am on Monday, 25 September 1978 there was a dry brittle explosion followed by a swirling cloud of black smoke that rose from the Korean capital's southern suburb of Yongdongpo.

This was the same troubled Asian peninsula where the Phantom had been an important fixture ever since times of much greater tension, the 1968–69 period when a virtual war had been going on. Now, tensions were as low as they could be in a divided nation where a million men under arms face each other across four kilometres of No Man's Land, and *this* Phantom loss was an operational one.

Two parachutes came down, the pilot and back-seater landing on the roof of the Panglim Spinning Company. The crew was safe but five people suffered burns at the crash scene near Korea's largest brewery (*not* nine killed, as a North Korean broadcast would assert the next day). Republic of Korea Air Force (ROKAF) F-4D-28-MC

Phantom 65-715, McAir ship 1764 had suffered an engine fire and had been lost—one of only four aircraft acknowledged to have been attrited in a service which has operated the type since August 1969.

The ROKAF first ordered 18 F-4Ds in 1968 during that tense period when North Korea was sending armed guerrillas into the south, firefights raged along the DMZ, and the crew of the US spy ship *Pueblo* was being held prisoner. A second batch of 18 F-4Ds followed, all taken from USAF inventory, all in camouflage with ROKAF markings, all stationed at Taegu. F-4Ds successfully intercepted a MiG-15 being flown into South Korean airspace by a defector on 6 December 1970.

Republic of Korea Air Force (ROKAF) F-4D Phantom (64-978) on hardstand at Taegu in 1976. The aircraft is armed with Bullpup air-to-surface missiles

Korean F-4E. F-4E-64-MC Phantom 76-495, McAir ship 4968, in flight on a mission from Taegu AB, Korea, on 19 February 1979. Fiscal year 1976 Phantoms delivered to Korea wore standard US Air Force camouflage while fiscal 1978 Phantoms were delivered in 'compass ghost' gray paint scheme (US Air Force)

OPPOSITE
The final St Louis airframe, F-4E Phantom (78-744) in US delivery markings and Compass Ghost gray camouflage, flying over Missouri in 1976, prior to delivery to the Republic of Korea Air Force. (See following page) (MDC)

The success of the F-4D type prompted Seoul to order 37 cannon-armed F-4Es from new production, these, too being stationed at Taegu. The first batch (76-493 to 76-511) was delivered in camouflage but the second (78-727 to 78-744) appeared in 'compass ghost' gray. The last of these, 78-744, the 5,068th Phantom, has been universally identified as the final St Louis F-4 but this does not take into account aircraft at least partially completed later for delivery to Iran. The ROKAF also had a strong interest in the RF-4E reconnaissance model but a purchase never materialized.

Korean Phantoms routinely exercise in company with US Air Force F-4Es assigned to the 51st Tactical Fighter Wing at Osan AB, Korea, during the periodic Team Spirit manoeuvres held in Korea—where friendly forces still operate under a United Nations mandate—and these operations have included dispersal landings and take-offs on reinforced sections of the Seoul-Pusan Highway. Given the density of the Korean combat theatre—the confrontation on the peninsula is a microcosm of the NATO/Warsaw Pact confrontation, and studies show North Korean forces capable of

attacking and winning *without* Soviet or Chinese help—alternate landing strips on reinforced roads are essential. The combined US/ROKAF Phantom force, bolstered by F-16s of the US 8th Tactical Fighter Wing's 'Wolfpack' at Kunsan AB, is heavily outnumbered by North Korea's force of 400 first-line tactical jets, including MiG-19s and MiG-21s.

A *tour d'horizon* of Phantom service under foreign flags is presented here. The full story, in volumes, probably cannot be told until the 21st century. But much of the following information has not appeared elsewhere.

Australia

As a stopgap measure during delays in its controversial order for the General Dynamics F-111C strike aircraft, the Royal Australian Air Force (RAAF) borrowed 24 F-4E Phantoms from USAF inventory. These were provided under Operation Peace Reef and the first machine, 69-304, arrived on 14 September 1970. The aircraft were assigned to 2 OCU and Nos 1 and 6 RAAF squadrons at Amberly. One machine, 69-7203,

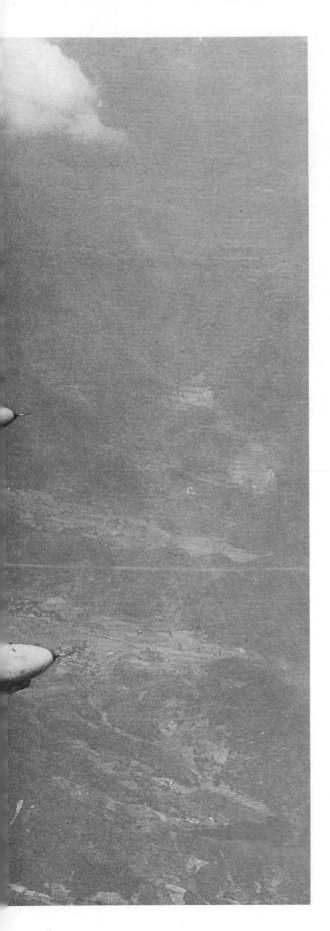

McAir ship 3856, crashed near Evans Head on 16 June 1971. Capt Bill Reiter, who now flies the F-4C for the Missouri Air National Guard in St Louis, was one of eight crewmembers from the 308th Tactical Fighter Squadron, Homestead AFB, Florida, who flew four of these aircraft from Brisbane RAAF Station back home to Hill AFB, Utah in November 1972. All surviving airframes, 23 in all, had been returned by 11 May 1973. An illustrative example, 69-7219, has since been converted to F-4G Advanced Wild Weasel standard and is now operated by the US Air Force's 37th Tactical Fighter Wing at George AFB, California.

Australian aircrews have since made effective use of the F-111C but they do not seem to feel toward it the same love that the Phantom often evokes. Says one, 'When I walk into the club, order a drink, and say I'm a 111 pilot, nobody looks up. When I walked into the club and said I'd just climbed out of a Phantom, everybody wanted to hear about it.'

Egypt

Anwar Sadat wanted the Phantom in a hurry for the 6 October 1979 National Day military parade, ironically the same event at which he would be assassinated three years later. President Jimmy Carter saw the Phantoms as symbolic of *rapprochement* with a nation earlier supplied with Russian equipment. So, under Operation Peace Pharaoh, at a cost of $594 million (£186 million), the US Air Force in 1979 supplied thirty-five F-4Es from its own stocks to the Air Force of the Arab Republic of Egypt.

All were early F-4Es, an illustrative example being 67-341, which had shot down a MiG-21 while serving with the 432nd Tactical Reconnaissance Wing in 1972.

No user has had worse luck with the Phantom. Ex-MiG pilots were rushed through training in the US but Egyptian maintenance personnel had no training at all. By October 1980, it was reported that only nine of the second-hand 'hangar queen' Phantoms were flying and their pilots were logging less than a dozen hours a week. Some returned to the US for repair, passing through RAF Alconbury, England, en route. The Cairo-West based fighters seem to have a limited future now that Egypt is having a more satisfactory experience with the newer F-16.

The final St Louis-manufactured machine, F-4E Phantom (78-744) is lead of four-ship formation of the Republic of Korea Air Force (ROKAF) in gray paint scheme with the silhouette of a lion on forward fuselage—a new insignia for Taegu-based F-4Es, adopted in 1983 (ROKAF)

Germany

Operation Peace Rhine was the generic US Air Force term for the delivery of Phantoms to Germany. The iron cross of the West German *Luftwaffe* first adorned a Phantom fuselage on 20 January 1971, when reconnaissance wing AKG-51 at Bremgarten received it first RF-4E. The 88 RF-4Es ordered by Bonn from 69-7448 (35 + 01) to 69-7535 (35 + 88), divided equally between AKG-51 and, since September 1971, AKG-52 at Leck.

F-4E Phantom 69-7208 with the 2nd Operational Conversion Unit, Royal Australian Air Force, upon its return from loan in May 1973. This machine was later converted to F-4G standard and is still active (Robert F Dorr)

BOTTOM LEFT
Two Egyptian F-4E Phantoms of the 222nd Fighter Regiment, Cairo West Airport, in slightly different low-visibility gray paint schemes in May 1983. Aircraft 66-375 in foreground is on jacks, indicating maintenance problems (Donald L Jay)

Luftwaffe F-4F Phantom 37 + 96 (72-1206) of JBG-35 based at Pfersfeld. This aircraft sports the current disruptive-splinter, two-tone grey camouflage scheme adopted by German air superiority Phantoms (Barry C Wheeler)

The success of the photo-reconnaissance Phantom led to the Federal Republic's order for 175 F-4F Phantoms. The F-4F, described in detail in chapter four, was conceived as an interceptor but the aircraft are now employed as fighter-bombers by JBG-35 at Pferdsfeld and JBG-36 at Hopsten while retaining the interceptor mission with JG-71, the fabled 'Richthofen' wing at Wittmundhafen and JG-74 at Neuberg. These aircraft were assigned serial numbers from 72-1111 (37 + 01) to 72-1285 (38 + 75). For a time in the early 1970s a dozen F-4Fs were stationed with the US Air Force's 35th Tactical Fighter Wing at George AFB, California, the training centre for German Phantom pilots, painted in standard West German splinter camouflage but with US markings and GA tailcodes. In more recent years, these aircraft have been returned to West Germany and, for greater commonality with US equipment, Bonn has purchased ten F-4E Phantoms from new production (75-628 through 75-637) for use at George, adorning them with US Air Force camouflage as well as markings. In the late 1970s, the *Luftwaffe* experimented with a variety of paint schemes for its F-4F fighters, finally deciding to replace the standard splinter camouflage with a lighter scheme of two-tone gray.

Greece

Although it has withdrawn from the NATO command structure, Greece's Hellenic Air Force, or *Helliniki Aeroporia*, remains committed to the defence of southern Europe and operates 62 Phantoms.

The 338th and 339th squadrons, or *mira*, operate the F-4E while an unidentified squadron flies the RF-4E, all three being assigned to the 117th group, or *pterighe*, of the HA's 28th Tactical Air Command, stationed at Andravidha.

Greece initially ordered 36 F-4Es in a procurement which required the personal approval of President Carter (72-1500 to 72-1535), obtained two more as replacements for aircraft lost by attrition (74-1618 and 74-1619) and later ordered an additional 18 (77-1743 to 77-1760). The HA's six reconnaissance Phantoms are 77-1761 to 77-1766. All of the HA aircraft come from new production and wear standard tactical camouflage with Greek national markings.

F-4E Phantom (72-1530) of the 338th Fighter Squadron, Hellenic Air Force, during a May 1979 visit by Greek Phantoms to the West German fighter base at Pfersfeld (Wieland Stoltze)

Iran

On a reconnaissance mission over South Yemen in 1977, an Iranian RF-4E was shot down by a rebel shoulder-mounted missile and went down in one fathom of crystal-clear gulf water where it can be seen easily from boats and aircraft. When the Iran–Iraq war broke out on 23 September 1980, an Iranian F-4E was destroyed on the ground at Tehran by strafing Iraqi aircraft. It was a bizarre-looking loss, the nose of the Phantom broken off like a bottle stem.

The Islamic Republic of Iran Air Force (IRIAF), serving the zealous Ayatollah's regime, then astounded everybody by getting a respectable number of its 227 Phantoms into battle and counter-assaulting Baghdad from the air.

The former Imperial Iranian Air Force (IIAF), or *Nirou Hayai Shahahanshahiye Iran*, has eleven Phantom squadrons (two F-4D, eight F-4E, one RF-4E) at Mehrabad, Shiraz and Tabriz. With the flow of US spare parts completely choked off and in the face of seemingly insurmountable difficulty in getting replacement parts—surprisingly, tyres proved the item most awkward to obtain and therefore first to cripple an otherwise airworthy craft—revolutionary Iran, reportedly with some clandestine assistance from Israel, has stupified Western intelligence analysts with its ability to 'keep 'em flying.'

Known to have borrowed at least two and perhaps several F-4Es from US Air Force

Iranian F-4D. On the ground in Tehran in August 1969 following delivery from the US, replete with centreline gun pod, is F-4D Phantom 67-14870, bearing local serial 3-602. This is the second of 32 F-4D models delivered to the Imperial Iranian Air Force (IIAF) (MDC)

inventory, Iran obtained from new production 32 F-4Ds (67-14869 through 67-14884; 68-6904 through 68-6919); 177 F-4Es (69-7711 through 69-7742; 71-1094 through 71-1166; 73-1519 through 73-1554; 75-222 through 75-257) and 16 reconnaissance RF-4Es (72-266 through 269; 74-1725 through 74-1736).

When revolution led to the cancellation of further orders, six further reconnaissance RF-4Es (78-751 through 78-754, 78-788 and 78-854) were very close to completion and are included in the figure for total Phantoms manufactured in this volume. The last-named would be the 5,074th St Louis-built Phantom and the final machine in McDonnell's production run (*not*, as universally published elsewhere, the 5,068th machine delivered as 78-744 to South Korea). Those six machines, described by one source as virtually complete airframes but by another as 'just bits and pieces of airplanes,' were for a time in storage in a hangar in St Louis and, legally, property of the US Air Force's Air Logistics Command. Some reports indicate that consideration was given to completing these aircraft and turning them over to the US Marine Corps to augment its aging RF-4B fleet. No clear picture exists as to whether it would have been practical to bring these RF-4Es up to full-fledged flying condition.

Around 1978, two events converged: (1) the previously reported decision personally taken by the elder chairman of the board, James S McDonnell, to stop soliciting new customers for the Phantom to free the company for newer projects, and (2) the overthrow of the Shah of Iran. At this time, a further 41 Phantoms were on order for Tehran which would have raised the McDonnell total to 5,115 (only ten of the 41 having reached the point of being assigned serials, 78-855 through 78-864) and would almost certainly have rendered more attractive purchases from other potential buyers such as Singapore—perhaps persuading the 'old man' to keep the line open, perhaps even through today. So it may have been the fervour of Islam which caused the end of the 22-year St Louis production run.

In early 1984, a curious rumour was in circulation that Spey turbofan engines had somehow been retrofitted on a number of the IRIAF's Phantoms. The British-manufactured Speys were supposedly being substituted for the familiar J79 to keep Iran's F-4s airworthy despite the absence of US support and spares. The Spey retrofit is a kind of major surgery, requiring new air intakes and a complete revision of the rear fuselage design, and it seems unlikely that any such transplant could have occurred without it being widely known. In any event, McDonnell Douglas had terminated its relationship with the Iranian authorities in February 1979 and Rolls-Royce, the originator of the Spey powerplant, strenuously denied supplying any of its engines to Tehran for installation in Phantoms. While re-engining is an important option in the Phantom's future (next chapter), it is exceedingly unlikely that Tehran would be ahead of the rest of the world in reaping the benefits.

This widely-published shot of a slatted F-4E over St Louis carrying an EROS collision-avoidance pod in the forward left Sparrow bay is not usually identified as Iranian. It is. F-4E Phantom 71-1139 is being 'shaken down' in trials at the manufacturer's facility immediately prior to delivery to the Imperial Iranian Air Force (IIAF) in 1977 (MDC)

Before the Shah was overthrown, it was the Imperial Iranian Air Force (IIAF). This is believed to be the first photo published in the West of an F-4D Phantom (67-14879) in the markings of the Islamic Republic of Iran Air Force (IRIAF)

Israel

With a chapter already devoted to the Israeli Air Force Defence Force (IDF/AF), it is appropriate only to mention here that Israel received 204 F-4E model aircraft. These included several batches from new production (68-396 to 68-547 with numerous gaps; 71-1779 through 71-1796; 74-1014 through 74-1037) plus those rushed to Israel from US Air Force inventory during the Yom Kippur War. The IDF/AF's twelve reconnaissance RF-4Es bore serial numbers 69-7590 through 69-7595 and 75-418 through 75-423.

Japan

The Japanese Air Self-Defense Force (JASDF) has five squadrons numbered 301-305 operating F-4E aircraft, also known as F-4EJ at Hyakuri, Chitose, Komatsu And Tsuiki. The first four airframes (17-8301 through 27-8304) were built by McDonnell. Nine more (27-8305 through 37-8313) came from the St Louis manufacturer as knockdown kits and were assembled in final form by Mitsubishi at Nagoya. Two further St Louis machines are listed As forward fuselage trials kits only (37-8314 and 37-8315) and were not assigned McAir ship numbers, although at least one of these has been observed flying as a complete aircraft. Mitsubishi then manufactured the remaining 125 JASDF aircraft (37-8316 through

17-8440), the last-named being the final Phantom built. In Japanese serial numbers, the first digit is the final digit of the year of *delivery* (37-8316 having been delivered in 1973) under the Western calendar, and the second digit simply identifies the aircraft type, 7 having been assigned to the Phantom. Because of the defensive role required by Japan's constitution, its F-4Es were originally delivered without air-to-air refuelling capability—a caution not observed when Japan later adopted the F-15J Eagle—but it is understood that this capacity has now been added.

Japan also operates 14 RF-4Es (47-6901 through 47-6914), these serving with the JASDF's 501 Squadron at Hyakuri.

Spain

Spain's Ala 12 wing at Torrejon operates 40 F-4C Phantoms (designated C.12 locally), of which four were provided as replacements for attrition, and four RF-4Cs (CR.12), all obtained from US Air Force inventory. Madrid is understood to be not fully satisfied with the Phantom type and plans to acquire further aircraft of the F-4E model were abandoned.

Turkey

Despite the 1974–1978 US embargo on arms sales arising from the Cyprus dispute, the Turkish Air Force or *Turk Hava Kuivvetleri* (THK) has become a major Phantom user with 95 machines in service and the likelihood that more will be acquired from US Air Force inventory. Spokesmen of both countries have made it absolutely clear that there is no truth to reports that Turkey would acquire, second-hand, the 35 F-4E Phantoms operated by Egypt.

TOP LEFT
Built in Nagoya, Mitsubishi F-4EJ Phantoms (57-8368, foreground) in flight over Japan in June 1977 (MDC)

BOTTOM LEFT
McDonnell-built RF-4E Phantom (57-6910) of the Japanese Air Self-Defense Force (JASDF) in June 1977 (MDC)

BELOW
McDonnell-built RF-4E Phantom (57-6900) of the Japanese Air Self-Defense Force (JASDF) in June 1978 (MDC)

*Last of the many, the final Phantom built, Mitsubishi F-
4EJ (17-8440) in temporary tactical camouflage lands with
parabrake in a snowy Japanese setting
(Toshiki Kudo)*

Spain obtained forty F-4Cs and four RF-4Cs. F-4C
Phantom 64-813, McAir ship 1141, with Spanish
designation C.12-13, belonging to the 122nd Squadron of
the 12th Wing is on approach at Torrejon—also a base for
US Air Force Phantoms of the 401st Tactical Fighter
Wing, in August 1973
(James T Sullivan)

BELOW
F-4E Phantom 73-1022 of the 7th Fighter Wing, Turkish
Air Force, based at Erhac Air Base, seen on a visit to
Villafrance, Italy, on 29 May 1981. Turkey does not
permit aviation photography, not even at the Air Force
museum
(Andre Wilderdijk)

Under Operation Peace Diamond III, the THK received 15 early F-4E direct from US Air Force holdings in 1974. Later, Ankara ordered 40 F-4Es from new production (73-1016 through 73-1055) and followed up with a further order for 32 F-4Es (77-277 through 77-308) and eight RF-4E reconnaissance machines (77-309 through 77-316). Acknowledged F-4E units are No 113 Sqn at Eskisehir and No 162 Sqn at Bandirma, both belonging to the THK's 1st Tactical Air Force which confronts the Soviet border under NATO auspices. There have been reports of 'close encounters' between Turkish Phantoms and Soviet MiG fighters, though no actual engagement is known to have taken place.

Fate selected a Turkish aircraft, 77-290, as the 5,000th Phantom delivered, concurrent with the 20th anniversary on 27 May 1978 of the first flight of the type. Robert C Little, now a Vice President of the McDonnell Douglas firm, veteran of that historic first flight in 142259 way back in 1958, went aloft in McAir ship 5,000 two decades later and pronounced it 'evidence of a quality product.'

Other Countries?

No Phantoms were ever supplied to the South Vietnamese Air Force and none belonging to the US were left behind when American forces withdrew from South Vietnam in early 1973. Numerous Phantoms, of course, were splattered across Thud Ridge and other embattled landmarks in North Vietnam—though none is ever known to have landed intact in Hanoi's territory. It must be assumed that the reunified Socialist Republic of Vietnam is in possession of numerous 'bits and pieces' of Phantoms but it is unlikely that any flyable airframe could have fallen into the former enemy's hands. Nor have there been reports of Iranian Phantoms falling into the possession of others following the Islamic revolution with its markedly anti-US flavour.

More than a decade after the end of the Vietnam fighting, three decades after the aircraft type was first conceived, the McDonnell F-4 Phantom remains too advanced, too complex, too sophisticated, for less developed Third World nations to make effective use of the aircraft. Further, with the exception of a hostile Iran, no current holder of the Phantom could transfer its airframes to another country without US permission and assistance.

Given time, however, history has its way of moving toward the inevitable. No US Air Force pilot of the 1940s would have believed that the Lockheed F-80 Shooting Star would end up serving in a half-dozen Latin American air forces. No jet jock of the 1950s would have suspected that the North American F-86 Sabre would finally grace the air arms of Ethiopia, Tunisia, and other once-unlikely users. But the day will come—as Phantoms are increasingly relegated to second-line duties in the industrialized states—when the F-4 may become a practical proposition for air arms in Asia, Africa, Latin America. No full list of foreign users of the proliferate St Louis product can be considered complete for years to come.

A final theme of speculation must be addressed towards the Peoples Republic of China, once such a staunch adversary of the US that even travel between the two nations was not permitted. In recent years, Beijing has had normalized diplomatic ties with Washington and has been a steady customer for advanced-technology items ranging from the Boeing 747 jetliner to satellite communications equipment. Political, legal and practical considerations still preclude any delivery of US military items to the Chinese, but a future resolution of the Taiwan issue could well lead to an American decision to supply an 'almost first-line' fighter from inventory. It is not totally farfetched to wonder if the final foreign users of the F-4 Phantom might not be the same Chinese pilots who once battled American fighters over MiG Alley before the Phantom was born.

Chapter 8
The Once and Future Phantom

Sit down, talk with Cdr Stan Grabber, executive officer of US Navy Reserve fighter squadron VF-201 at NAS Dallas, Texas. Any notion that the Phantom is past history will be quickly, emphatically dispelled. 'This one is a formidable fighting machine in the mid-1980s,' says Stan of the F-4S Phantoms his squadron received to replace the F-4N in December 1983. Grabber should know, with two Vietnam combat cruises under his belt. Get past the man's lively humour—'We once had a RIO who was an ordained minister and was in great demand as a flying partner because of his connections'—and Grabber is serious. Other men in Navy and Marine Corps uniform acknowledge that their Phantoms will be land-based from here out—except for *Midway*, carrier decks are the province of the Grumman F-14 Tomcat—but they do not see the McDonnell machine going to the boneyard any time soon. Says Lt Melvin Pobre of VF-201: 'We think the Phantom can still take on the best in the world and win.'

Fight and win. If it is no longer the first-line fighter in all of the dozen-odd air forces it serves, the F-4 Phantom can still argue for recognition as

Near Okinawa in 1978, F-4J Phantom 155740, coded NF-111, of the 'Chargers' of VF-161 from USS Midway *(CVA-41) formates with an AV-8A Harrier. Midway Phantoms scored the first and last MiG kills of the Vietnam war. Homeported at Yokosuka, Japan, the only American carrier ported outside the US,* Midway *will also be the last carrier to operate the Phantom. Its squadrons, VF-151 and VF-161, now operate the F-4S model (US Navy)*

OVERLEAF
Guarding American skies in the mid-1980s are veteran F-4C Phantoms of the 184th Tactical Fighter Squadron, Arkansas Air National Guard, seen escorting a Boeing B-52G Stratofortress. These Phantoms are stationed at Fort Smith, Arkansas (Don Spering)

the most important military aircraft type outside the Soviet Union. Around 3,000 remain in service. The US Air Force and Air National Guard fleet of Phantoms has accumulated nine million flight hours since 1963 and has had major accidents at the rate of 6.4 per 100,000 flight hours—a respectable figure but not a superlative one. This fleet currently accomplishes 330,000 flying hours per year by flying about 20,000 sorties per month. Maintenance experience has been generally very favourable for an aircraft type which remains unusually complex, the Phantom being so intricate that it has 510 individual lubrication points, 281 fuel link connections, 900 individual electrical connectors and 294 avionics units.

Programmes to extend the service life of the Phantom have already been described. These produced the US Air Force F-4G Wild Weasel and the US Navy F-4N and F-4S—all models which never existed on the manufacturer's drawing boards or production line. But even without major rebuild, Phantoms are continually being repaired, updated, improved. A current example is a $2.74 million (£1.93 million) contract let to the Boeing Military Airplane Company in Wichita, Kansas for depot maintainance of F-4C Phantoms operated by the Air Force Reserve and Air National Guard. 'This is a measure of the confidence we have in the future operational value of the design,' says an Air Force officer. In 1984–5, the Wichita facility was to work on 86 F-4C airframes performing inspection for corrosion and metal fatigue and repairing and overhauling equipment, including ejection seats. The first F-4C to emerge from this process was delivered in March 1984 to the 181st Tactical Fighter Group, Indiana Air National Guard, stationed at Terre Haute, Indiana.

The generally favourable record of all the world's Phantoms is a tribute to the General Electric J79 engine, first flown in 1955, originally

TOP LEFT
Air Combat fighter in the 1980s. The F-4E Phantom remains a first-line fighter with the 347th Tactical Fighter Wing at Moody AFB, Georgia. The wing has a commitment to Middle East operations and has flown in Egypt as part of manoeuvres by the Rapid Deployment Joint Task Force (RDJTF). F-4E Phantom 68-369, coded MY, has patriotic colours on the fin of its centreline tow target at the William Tell gunnery meet, Tyndall AFB, Florida, in October 1982. But wraparound camouflage, black tail-codes and black national insignia are an early 1980's measure to reduce visibility to the enemy in the air combat arena

BOTTOM LEFT
Considered by many the cradle of American fighter aviation, Nellis Air Force Base near Las Vegas, Nevada is the home of 'Red Flag' air combat training and of fighter development work. F-4E Phantom 74-648 of Nellis' 57th Fighter Weapons Wing, coded WA, was used for tactics development and is seen in November 1978 after wraparound camouflage was adopted but before white tailcodes were changed to black. Unit was subsequently redesignated 57th Tactical Training Wing (Paul Bennett)

'Wild Weasel' F-4G Phantom electronic warfare aircraft carrying its full portfolio of toolery—Shrike, Standard ARM, Pave Spike, Maverick, Harm—on mission with 37th Tactical Fighter Wing. In 1984, US Air Force made decision to integrate F-4Gs into fighter squadrons rather than operating discreet squadrons of F-4G aircraft (MDC)

179

chosen for the now-retired Convair B-58 Hustler and North American A3J Vigilante, and still 'going strong.' In its time, the J79 was a breakthrough, solving the need for a high-ratio compressor by using a single high-pressure rotor with upstream rows of intermediate stator blades, which are fixed on other powerplants, in adjustable rows, able to be pivoted to exactly the right angular setting for the airflow. Also adopted for the Lockheed F-104 Starfighter, the J79 is a remarkably efficient power source in all regions of the aircraft's performance envelope and has shown enormous stretching potential over the years. Although future development of the seemingly timeless Phantom airframe may depend upon re-engining for service beyond the year 2000, the importance of the J79 over a quarter-century cannot be over-emphasized. The engine is what gets it there. The Phantom's effectiveness as a weapon comes in part from its enormous versatility and development potential. And the Phantom seems capable of handling any new ordnance that comes along. A remarkably innovative example, tested with West Germany's F-4Fs, is a Messerschmitt-Boelkow-Blohm (MBB) anti-armour weapon, ideal for NATO, which uses pod-mounted sensors to locate and identify targets without pilot intervention. The system then fires an unguided munition to the rear at an inclined angle resulting in a vertical trajectory that impacts on top of the target. The day may come when a re-engined F-4F Phantom uses the MBB weapon to strike at invading Soviet/Warsaw Pact tank columns on the plains of Western Europe.

While the US Air Force, Navy and Marine Corps give less priority to improving their Phantoms than to purchasing newer F-14s, F-16s and F/A-18s, other nations which operate the Phantom see enormous stretching potential in the design. Of several countries seeking to capitalize on the Phantom's potential—while relying still upon the proven J79 engine rather than electing the costly step of installing a new powerplant—none has moved faster than Japan.

Though committed to a solely defensive posture since World War II, Tokyo has become increasingly aware of the Soviet threat to its northwest as well as the ever-lingering risk of hostilities on the nearby Korean peninsula. By the time this is printed, Japan will be test-flying in

Ceremonies at St Louis on 7 July 1965 mark roll-out of the 1,000th Phantom. Displayed for the occasion are, from right to left, RF-4B 151977 (McAir ship 777) painted as Phantom number 999, F-4B 152276 (McAir ship 1034) painted as number 1,000 and F-4C 64-769 (McAir ship 1063) painted as number 1,001. While this is a superb exhibit of variants in production at the time, the real Phantom number 999 was F-4C 64-728, number 1,000 was F-4C 64-729, and number 1,001 was RF-4C 64-1058 (MDC)

Typical of Phantoms serving with Air National Guard (ANG) units in defence of North America is this F-4C-21-MC aircraft 64-660 of the 136th Fighter Interceptor Squadron, 107th Fighter Interceptor Group, New York Air National Guard, Niagara Falls, NY. This F-4C is also a triple MiG killer from the Rolling Thunder operations, having shot down three MiG-17s, one with an AIM-7 Sparrow and two with 20-mm guns mounted in SUU/16 gun pods
(Don Linn)

OPPOSITE PAGE
Aircrew prepare to take delivery of the 2,000th Phantom at St Louis, on 12 March 1967. Actually, aircraft is F-4D Phantom 66-7533, McAir ship 2062. The real 2,000th Phantom was a different F-4D, 66-7489
(MDC)

early 1985 a single F-4EJ airframe modified extensively to test the limits of the Phantom's performance envelope. The modified Japanese machine will introduce Westinghouse APG-66 radar, an advanced Litton inertial navigation system, Kaiser-built head-up display (HUD) and a locally manufactured radar homing and early warning system (RHAWS) receiver. The enhanced Japanese Phantom, costing about $5 million (£3.3 million) not including the initial investment in the

machine, will be able to employ AIM-7F Sparrow air-to-air SARH and AIM-9L Sidewinder IR missiles as well as Type 80 anti-shipping missiles. If the testbed airframe is successful, notwithstanding the already heavy commitment made to the F-15J Eagle, most of Japan's F-4EJ Phantoms could be modified to the new standard beginning in 1988.

The Super Phantom

A provocative offer to broaden the Phantom's future was made jointly by Boeing and Pratt & Whitney in 1984. Here, the idea of re-engining the F-4 design assumes paramount importance and the 20,000-lb (9,070-kg) thrust Pratt & Whitney PW1120 turbojet engine is critical to the proposal—although the plan would be lacking in realism without other features to update the Phantom for the 1990s. In addition to new engines, the Boeing Super Phantom would have state-of-the-art avionics, new head-up display (HUD), an under-fuselage conformal fuel tank (CFT) and ALE-40 flare/chaff dispenser. The

OPPOSITE
'The Evaluators' of VX-4 at NAS Point Mugu, California have flown some oddly-painted Phantoms. 'Black Bunny' in background (153783) is well known. Rarely seen is F-4J Phantom (155896) in foreground with experimental blue-gray camouflage scheme (MDC)

Defender of NATO's northern flank. The F-4E still serves as a front-line interceptor with the 57th Fighter Interceptor Squadron at Keflavik AB, Iceland, which routinely intercepts and escorts Soviet bombers and intelligence-gathering aircraft. F-4E Phantom 66-334 in the gray paint scheme used for air defence aircraft, shadows a Bear (Paul Bennett)

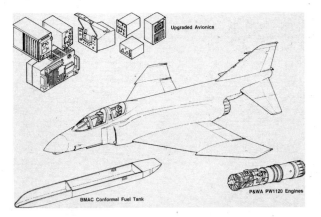

Drawing released in March 1984 by the Boeing Military Airplane Company, Wichita, Kansas, shows key features of the proposed, re-engined 'Super Phantom'. Rebuilt aircraft would have Pratt & Whitney PW1120 engines, an under-fuselage conformal fuel tank, and updated avionics equipment

OPPOSITE
The US Air Force's flight demonstration team The Thunderbirds, of the 4510th Air Demonstration Squadron at Nellis AFB, Nevada, operated early, unslatted F-4E Phantoms until an economy move by the Carter administration shifted the team into Northrop T-38. More recently, the Thunderbirds have flown the General Dynamics F-16 Fighting Falcon
(US Air Force)

conformal fuel tank, says Boeing, will reduce drag 29 per cent and add 37 per cent more fuel for increased range.

Re-engining the Phantom with the lighter Pratt & Whitney PW1120 will sharply improve the fighter's air combat performance. Boeing figures show a new thrust-to-weight ratio of 1.03 to 1, exceeding unity for the first time—compared, the company says, to 0.89 for the J79-powered Phantom, 0.75 for the MiG-21 and 0.73 for the MiG-23. This, says the maker, would permit 13 per cent tighter turns at high altitude and would reduce take off roll from 3,300 ft to 2,600 ft (1,006 m 792 m). The re-engined Phantom, it is claimed, would significantly reduce maintenance man-hours.

Boeing—again, the firm's Wichita, Kansas military facility—has proposed flying a PW1120-powered Phantom testbed under a programme costing $16 million (£10.75 million) and says the first aircraft could be aloft by the end of 1985. As noted earlier, the US armed services appear unenthusiastic—the Marine Corps may prove an exception—preferring to invest in newer aircraft types. But the foreign market is lucrative. Richard DeLauer, Under Secretary of Defense for Research and Engineering, actively supports the proposal for America's foreign allies, with West Germany and South Korea reportedly especially interested in the Super Phantom proposal. Turkey is also a likely customer but appears less able to field the investment. Allen F Hobbs of Boeing is

US Navy's Blue Angels flight demonstration team in F-4J
Phantoms before a Carter administration economy move
shifted them to A-4F Skyhawks

TOP LEFT
Members of the US Air Force's Thunderbirds flight
demonstration team pose in front of one of the F-4E
Phantoms operated by the team during the 1970s
(US Air Force)

OPPOSITE
The US Navy's Blue Angels flight demonstration team
usually puts on a good show, but not this way. F-4J
Phantom (153085) bellied-in on fire at Cedar Rapids,
Iowa, 30 August 1970. The pilot made a successful zero-
zero ejection shortly after striking concrete
(Dick Gerdes)

said to believe that a firm market exists for 300 to 500 Super Phantom airframes in the late 1980s and early 1990s. Some US officers, while recognizing that American forces will not underwrite the full costs of the programme, are arguing, nevertheless, that the US services should shed their reluctance and capitalize on a common upgrade in company with other nations.

Two Super Phantom test-beds were scheduled to fly in 1985, one for the US Air Force (solely to test the system for foreign sales) and one for Israel.

Other Futures

As this century nears its end, Phantom airframes may find other uses and earn new designations. A US Navy Wild Weasel Phantom is not an unrealistic prospect. The US Air Force may develop further its own F-4G Advanced Wild Weasel which plays such a critical role in the electronic warfare theatre and serves from Spangdahlem AB, Germany to Clark Field in the Philippines. As the Navy has already done with the QF-4B and QF-4N, the US Air Force may well elect its own target drone version to enhance its current fleet of North American QF-100 Super Sabres and Convair PQM-102 Delta Daggers.

Meanwhile, at the front lines where warriors still stand ready to move in when policymakers need them, men born at the same time as the Phantom fly the aircraft knowing that at any moment they may have to take it back into battle—perhaps against new Soviet fighter types like the MiG-31, perhaps in a nuclear or chemical battle environment. Guy Walsh was born around

the time Herman Barkey and his McDonnell design team were roughing out the first sketches of the Phantom. In his spare time, Walsh studies international relations, and knows that nations will always need the men and machines to fly and fight. Fulltime, Capt Guy Walsh, only recently elevated from first lieutenant, is an RF-4C pilot with Lt Col Donald S Pickard's 1st Tactical Reconnaissance Squadron at RAF Alconbury, England. At a bull session in the squadron briefing room, North Vietnam drawn out in chalk on a green board, when Pickard and Lt Col Greg Bailey point at the crude map and rap about lessons learned in the RF-4C over Route Package Six in May 1972, they are discussing something that happened when Walsh was fifteen years old. Behind barbed wire, near the protective gear kept on hand for chemical warfare, inside a reinforced Tab-Vee hangar designed to withstand a direct hit from a 500-lb (227-kg) bomb, Walsh's RF-4C sits in wraparound camouflage and black tailcodes— ready. Almost as old as he is, Walsh's RF-4C has been reconfigured and has changed almost as much as he has since both were conceived. Near his aircraft is a sign: THE MISSION OF THE UNITED STATES AIR FORCE IS TO FLY AND FIGHT, AND DON'T YOU EVER FORGET IT. In an aircraft which many now consider old, is Walsh ready to do battle if he has to? We study the machine together, warrior and diplomat. The thought is mine, the one about how often brave men in fighter cockpits must take over the job from old men at the negotiating table. 'We're here to get it done right,' Guy Walsh utters. He doesn't say much either.

Abbreviations

AFB—Air Force Base
CAP Combat Air Patrol
Capt—Captain
Cdr—Commander
CO—Commanding Officer
Col—Colonel
CV; CVA; CVN—Fleet Carrier; Attack Carrier; Nuclear Carrier
DMZ—Demilitarized Zone
ECM—Electronic Countermeasures
G—one gravity force
GIB—Guy in back. The pilot systems officer (PSO) in the back seat of F-4C, RF-4C and F-4D circa 1962–1968
IAS—Indicated Air Speed
in—inches
jg—junior grade
km; km/hr—kilometre; km per hour
lb—pounds
lit—litres
Lt—Lieutenant
Lt Cdr—Lieutenant Commander
Lt Col-Lieutenant Colonel
1/Lt—First Lieutenant

Maj—Major
McAir—McDonnell Aircraft Corporation
MCAS—Marine Corps Air Station
m—metre
mph—miles per hour
NASA—National Aeronautics and Space Administration
NATO—North Atlantic Treaty Organization
NVA—North Vietnamese Army, ie the regular forces of North Vietnam as opposed to Viet Cong forces in South Vietnam
OCU—Operational Conversion Unit
POL—Petroleum/Oil/Lubricant. The term used for oil supplies held in storage
POW—Prisoner of War
RAG—Replacement Air Group. The landbased naval Phantom unit assigned to support carrier-based squadrons
RIO—Radar Intercept Officer. Back-seat crew member in US Navy and US Marine Corps Phantoms
RPM—revolutions per minute
SAM—Surface-to-Air Missile
TACAN—Tactical Air Navigation System
WSO—Weapons Systems Officer. The back-seater in US Air Force Phantoms from about 1968 onwards

Specifications

The First and the Last

	F4H-1 142259 St Louis, Missouri 27 May 1958	F-4EJ 17-8440 Nagoya, Japan 31 March 1984
Length	58 ft 1 in (17.70 m)	63 ft (19.20 m)
Wing span	38 ft 5 in (11.70 m)	38 ft 5 in (11.70 m)
Wing area	530 ft^2 (49.2 m^2)	530 ft^2 (49.2 m^2)
Height	16 ft 3 in (4.96 m)	16 ft 3 in (4.96 m)
Empty weight	27,640 lb (12,535 kg)	29,675 lb (13,458 kg)
Maximum weight	54,600 lb (24, 761 kg)	59,640 lb (27,047 kg)
Powerplant	J79-GE-2	J79-ITI-17
Thrust	16,150 lb (7,324 kg)	17,900 lb (8,120 kg)
Armament	4 × AIM-7*	4 × AIM-7
	4 × AIM-9*	4 × AIM-9
Fire control radar	APQ-50*	APQ-120
Bombing system	AJB-3	AJB-7

*Not actually installed on prototype

Appendices

Appendix 1. **F-4 Phantoms manufactured**

Model	Amount	From	To	Remarks
F-4A	2	142259	142260	Formerly F4H-1; F4H-1F
	5	143388	143392	Conversions to TF-4A
	11	145307	145317	
	5	146817	146821	
	24	148252	148275	
Subtotal	47			
F-4B	72	148363	148434	2 modified to YRF-4C
	72	149403	149474	12 built as F-4G
	88	150406	150493	44 converted to QF-4B
	30	150624	150653	228 converted to F-4N
	29	150993	151021	
	123	151397	151519	
	125	152207	152331	
	106	152965	153070	
	4	153912	153915	
	2	62-12200	62-12201	
Subtotal	651			
RF-4B	9	151975	151983	Formerly F4H-1P
	27	153089	153115	
	10	157342	157351	
Subtotal	46			
F-4C	1	62-12199		Formerly F-110A
	307	63-7407	63-7713	40 transferred to Spain
	275	64-654	64-928	36 converted to Wild Weasel
Subtotal	583			
Model	Amount	From	To	Remarks
RF-4C	24	63-7740	63-7763	Formerly RF-110A
	89	64-997	64-1085	4 transferred to Spain
	128	65-818	65-945	1 loaned to Israel
	96	66-383	66-478	
	42	67-428	67-469	
	64	68-548	68-611	
	36	69-349	69-384	
	12	71-248	71-259	
	12	72-145	72-156	
Subtotal	503			
F-4D	52	64-929	64-980	36 transferred to Korea
	222	65-580	65-801	
	58	66-226	66-283	

Model	Amount	From	To	Remarks
	320	66-7455	66-7774	
	141	66-8685	66-8825	
	16	67-14869	67-14884	Iran
	16	68-6904	68-6919	
Subtotal	*825*			
F-4E	99	66-284	66-382	116 converted to F-4G
	191	67-208	67-398	Conversions to F-4P
	245	68-303	68-547	Transfers to Israel, Egypt, Turkey
	72	69-236	69-307	
	103	69-7201	69-7303	Loans to Israel, Iran
	44	69-7546	69-7589	
	24	71-224	71-247	
	24	71-1070	71-1093	
	12	71-1391	71-1402	
	24	72-121	72-144	
	12	72-157	72-168	
	1	72-1407		
	24	72-1476	72-1499	
	48	73-1157	73-1204	
	24	74-643	74-666	
	24	74-1038	74-1061	
	34	74-1620	74-1653	
	10	75-628	75-637	West Germany
	36	72-1500	72-1535	Greece
	2	74-1618	74-1619	Greece
	18	77-1743	77-1760	Greece
	32	69-7711	69-7742	Iran
	73	71-1094	71-1166	Iran
	36	73-1519	73-1554	Iran
	36	75-222	75-257	Iran
	18	71-1779	71-1796	Israel
	24	74-1014	74-1037	Israel
	19	76-493	76-511	South Korea
	18	78-727	78-744	South Korea
	40	73-1016	73-1055	Turkey
	32	77-277	77-308	Turkey
	15	17-8301	37-8315	Japan
Subtotal	*1,397*			
Model	Amount	From	To	Remarks
RF-4E	88	69-7448	69-7535	West Germany (35+01 to 35+88)
	6	77-1761	77-1766	Greece
	4	72-266	72-269	Iran
	12	74-1725	74-1736	Iran
	4	78-751	78-754	Iran
	1	78-788		Iran
	1	78-854		Iran
	6	69-7590	69-7595	Israel
	6	75-418	75-423	Israel
	8	77-309	77-316	Turkey
	14	47-6901	57-6914	Japan
Subtotal	*150*			
F-4F	175	72-1111	72-1285	West Germany (37+01 to 38+75)
Subtotal	*175*			
F-4J	18	153071	153088	Conversions to F-4S
	144	153768	153911	15 transferred to RAF
	8	154781	154788	
	77	155504	155580	
	173	155731	155903	
	68	157242	157309	
	34	158346	158379	
Subtotal	*502*			
Model	Amount	From	To	Remarks
YF-4K	2	XT595	XT596	
Subtotal	*2*			

Model	Amount	From	To	Remarks
F-4K	2	XT597	XT598	
	20	XT857	XT876	
	28	XV565	XV592	
Subtotal	50			
YF-4M	2	XT852	XT853	
Subtotal	2			
F-4M	24	XT891	XT914	
	50	XV393	XV442	
	42	XV460	XV501	
Subtotal	116			
F-4EJ	125	37-8316	17-8440	Manufactured by Mitsubishi
Subtotal	125			
Total	5,201			

Appendix 2. **US Air Force Phantom Units**

US Air Force, Air Force Reserve (AFRes) and Air National Guard (ANG) units operating the F-4 Phantom as of 31 March 1984.

Unit	Location	Type	Tailcode
Air Force Logistics Command			
Ogden ALC	Ogden AFB, Utah	F-4C, RF-4C	None
Air Force Systems Command			
3246 TW	Eglin AFB, Florida	F-4C, F-4D, F-4E	AD
6512 TS	Edwards AFB, Calif	RF-4C, F-4D, F-4E	ED
Pacific Air Forces (PACAF)			
3 TFW	Clark AB, Phillipines	F-4E, F-4G	PN
18 TFW	Kadena AB, Okinawa	RF-4C	ZZ
51 TFW	Osan AB, Korea	F-4E	OS
Tactical Air Command (TAC)			
4 TFW	Seymour Johnson AFB, NC	F-4E	SJ
31 TFW	Homestead AFB, Florida	F-4D	ZF
35 TFW	George AFB, Calif	F-4E	GA
37 TFW	George AFB, Calif	F-4E, F-4G	WW
57 FWW	Nellis AFB, Nevada	F-4E	WA
67 TRW	Bergstrom AFB, Texas	RF-4C	BA
347 TFW	Moody AFB, Georgia	F-4E	MY
363 TFW	Shaw AFB, SC	RF-4C	SW
57 FIS	Keflavik AB, Iceland	F-4E	None
4485 TS	Eglin AFB, FLorida	F-4E, F-4G	OT
US Air Forces in Europe (USAFE)			
10 TRW	RAF Alconbury, England	RF-4C	AR
26 TRW	Zweibrucken AB, Germany	RF-4C	ZR
52 TFW	Spangdahlem AB, Germany	F-4E, F-4G	SP
86 TFW	Ramstein AB, Germany	F-4E	RS
401 TFW	Torrejon AB, Spain	F-4D	TJ
Air Force Reserve (AFRES)			
89 TFS 906 TFG	Dayton, Ohio	F-4D	DO
93 TFS 482 TFW	Homestead AFB Fla	F-4D	FM
457 TFS 301 TFW	Carswell AFB, Tx	F-4D	TH
465 TFS 507 TFG	Tinker AFB, Okla	F-4D	SH
704 TFS 924 TFG	Bergstrom AFB, Tx	F-4D	TX
Air National Guard (ANG)			
106 TRS 117 TRW	Birmingham, Alabama	RF-4C	None
110 TFS 131 TFW	St Louis, Missouri	F-4C	SL
111 FIS 147 FIG	Ellington AFB, Texas	F-4C	None
113 TFS 181 TFG	Terre Haute, Indiana	F-4C	HF
121 TFS 113 TFW	Andrews, AFB, Maryland	F-4D	DC
122 TFS 159 TFG	NAS New Orleans, La	F-4C	None
123 FIS 142 FIG	Portland, Oregon	F-4C	None
127 TFTS 184 TFTG	McConnell AFB, Kansas	F-4D	None
128 TFS 116 TFW	Dobbins AFB, Georgia	F-4D	None
134 TFS 158 TFG	Burlington, Vermont	F-4D	VT

Unit	Location	Type	Tailcode
136 FIS 107 FIG	Niagara Falls, NY	F-4C	None
141 TFS 108 TFW	McGuire AFB, NJ	F-4D	NJ
153 TRS 186 TRG	Meridian, Mississippi	RF-4C	KE
160 TRS 187 TRG	Montgomery, Alabama	RF-4C	None
163 TFS 122 TFW	Fort Wayne, Indiana	F-4C	FW
165 TRS 123 TRW	Louisville, Kentucky	RF-4C	KY
170 TFS 183 TFG	Springfield, Illinois	F-4D	None
171 FIS 191 FIG	Selfridge, Michigan	F-4C	None
173 TRS 155 TRG	Lincoln, Nebraska	RF-4C	None
178 FIS 119 FIG	Fargo, North Dakota	F-4D	None
179 TRS 148 TRG	Duluth, Minnesota	RF-4C	None
182 TFS 149 TFG	Kelly AFB, Texas	F-4C	SA
184 TFS 188 TFG	Fort Smith, Arkansas	F-4C	None
190 TRS 124 TRG	Boise, Idaho	RF-4C	None
192 TRS 152 TRG	Reno, Nevada	RF-4C	None
196 TFS 163 TFG	March AFB, Calif	F-4C	None
199 FIS 154 TFG	Hickam AFB, Hawaii	F-4C	None

Appendix 3. US Navy F-4 Phantom Fighter Squadrons

US Navy fighter squadrons, still designated under an ancient system whereby 'V' means heavier-than-air and 'F' means fighter, shift from land bases to carrier air wings, and change tailcodes according to air wing assignments. The following are the principal squadrons which have operated the F-4 Phantom.

Squadron	Nickname	Traditional Home Port
VF-11	Red Rippers	NAS Oceana, Virginia
VF-14	Tophatters	NAS Oceana, Virginia
VR-21	Freelancers	NAS Miramar, California
VF-22L1	None	NAS Alameda, California
VF-31	Tomcatters	NAS Oceana, Virginia
VF-32	Swordsmen	NAS Oceana, Virginia
VF-33	Tarsiers	NAS Oceana, Virginia
VF-41	Black Aces	NAS Miramar, California
VF-51	Screaming Eagles	NAS Miramar, California
VF-74	Be-Devilers	NAS Oceana, Virginia
VF-84	Jolly Rogers	NAS Oceana, Virginia
VF-92	Silver Kites	NAS Miramar, California
VF-96	Fighting Falcons	NAS Miramar, California
VF-101	Grim Reapers	NAS Oceana, Virginia
VF-102	Diamondbacks	NAS Oceana, Virginia
VF-103	Sluggers	NAS Oceana, Virginia
VF-111	Sundowners	NAS Miramar, California
VF-114	Aardvarks	NAS Miramar, California
VF-121	Pacemakers	NAS Miramar, California
VF-142	Ghostriders	NAS Miramar, California
VF-143	Pukin Dogs	NAS Miramar, California
VF-151	Fighting Vigilantes	NAF Atsugi, Japan
VF-154	Black Knights	NAS Miramar, California
VF-161	Chargers	NAF Atsugi, Japan
VF-171	Aces	NAS Oceana, Virginia
VF-191	Satan's Kittens	NAS Miramar, California
VF-194	Hellfires	NAS Miramar, California
VF-201	Rangers	NAS Dallas, Texas
VF-202	Superheats	NAS Dallas, Texas
VF-213	Black Lions	NAS Miramar, California
VF-301	Devil's Disciples	NAS Miramar, California
VF-302	Stallions	NAS Miramar, California
VAQ-33	Hunters	NAS Norfolk, Virginia
VX-4	Evaluators	NAS Point Mugu, California

Appendix 4. **US Marine Corps F-4 Phantom Squadrons**

Three Marine Aircraft Wings, one for each Marine ground division, are headquartered at Cherry Point, North Carolina; El Toro, California, and Iwakuni, Japan. Marine fighter attack squadrons often shift from one aircraft wing to another but retain a permanently assigned tailcode except on rare occasion when embarked shipboard with a US Navy carrier air wing. The following are the principal Marine squadrons which have operated the F-4 Phantom.

Squadron	Nickname	Tailcode	Traditional Base
VMFAT-101	Sharpshooters	SH	MCAS Yuma, Arizona
VMFA-112	Wolf Pack	MA	NAS Dallas, Texas
VMFA-115	Silver Eagles	VE	MCAS Beaufort, SC
VMFA-122	Crusaders	DC	MCAS Beaufort, SC
VMFAT-201	None	KB	MCAS Cherry Point, NC
VMFA-212	Lancers	WB	MCAS Kaneohe Bay, Hawaii
VMFA-232	Red Devils	WT	MCAS Iwakuni, Japan
VMFA-235	Death Angels	DB	MCAS Kaneohe Bay, Hawaii
VMFA-251	Thunderbolts	DW	MCAS Beaufort, SC
VMFA-312	Checkerboards	DR	MCAS Beaufort, SC
VMFA-314	Black Knights	VW	MCAS El Toro, California
VMFA-321	Hell's Angeles	MG	Andrews AFB, Maryland
VMFA-323	Death Rattlers	WS	MCAS El Toro, California
VMFA-333	Shamrocks	DN	MCAS Beaufort, SC
VMFA-334	Falcons	WU	MCAS El Toro, California
VMFA-351	None	MC	NAF Atlanta, Georgia
VMFA-451	Warlords	VM	MCAS Beaufort, SC
VMFA-513	Flying Nightmares	WF	MCAS El Toro, California
VMFA-531	Gray Ghosts	EC	MCAS Cherry Point, NC
VMFA-542	Bengals	WH	MCAS El Toro, California
VMCJ-1	None	RM	MCAS Iwakuni, Japan
VMCJ-2	Playboys	CY	MCAS Cherry Point, NC
VMCJ-3	None	TN	MCAS El Toro, California
VMFP-3	Eyes of the Corps	RF	MCAS El Toro, California

Index